# MORE THAN A MOMENT

# MORE THAN A MOMENT

*Contextualizing the Past, Present,*
*and Future of MOOCs*

STEVEN D. KRAUSE

UTAH STATE UNIVERSITY PRESS
*Logan*

© 2019 by University Press of Colorado

Published by Utah State University Press
An imprint of University Press of Colorado
245 Century Circle, Suite 202
Louisville, Colorado 80027

 The University Press of Colorado is a proud member of
the Association of University Presses.

The University Press of Colorado is a cooperative publishing enterprise supported, in part, by Adams State University, Colorado State University, Fort Lewis College, Metropolitan State University of Denver, Regis University, University of Colorado, University of Northern Colorado, University of Wyoming, Utah State University, and Western Colorado University.

∞ This paper meets the requirements of the ANSI/NISO Z39.48–1992 (Permanence of Paper)

ISBN: 978-1-60732-786-8 (paperback)
ISBN: 978-1-60732-787-5 (ebook)
https://doi.org/10.7330/9781607327875

Library of Congress Cataloging-in-Publication Data

Names: Krause, Steven D., author.
Title: More than a moment : contextualizing the past, present, and future of MOOCs / Steven Krause.
Description: Logan : Utah State University Press, [2019] | Includes bibliographical references and index.
Identifiers: LCCN 2019033198 (print) | LCCN 2019033199 (ebook) | ISBN 9781607327868 (paperback) | ISBN 9781607327875 (ebook)
Subjects: LCSH: MOOCs (Web-based instruction) | Education, Higher—Effect of technological innovations on.
Classification: LCC LB1044.87 (print) | LCC LB1044.87 (ebook) | DDC 371.33/44678—dc23
LC record available at https://lccn.loc.gov/2019033198
LC ebook record available at https://lccn.loc.gov/2019033199

# CONTENTS

# ACKNOWLEDGMENTS

First and foremost, I want to thank Annette Wannamaker. Annette is my wife (and thus my love, my best friend, and my life partner in all things), but she is also an incredibly skilled writer, editor, and scholar. Her encouragement, support, and on-the-page suggestions helped shape this project. Without Annette, I'm not sure this book would have happened. Thank you, my dear.

Thanks to my friend and colleague John Mauk, also an excellent scholar and teacher, whose feedback on one of the later drafts of this project was invaluable and encouraging. Thanks to the anonymous reviewers of this book in manuscript, especially the detailed and pointed critiques of "reviewer one" wherever and whoever you are. My thanks to all of my Eastern Michigan University colleagues for their thoughts and support and ideas (along with putting up with me on a day-to-day basis), particularly Derek Mueller, Steve Benninghoff, John Dunn, Chalice Randazzo, Rachel Gramer, and Logan Bearden. Thanks as well to EMU for supporting me with a sabbatical and a faculty research fellowship, support that made this project possible.

My journey through the MOOC moment before this book helped me connect with great writers and scholars from all over the world. Thanks to Charles Lowe and David Blakesley for the project that laid the groundwork for this one, *Invasion of the MOOCs: The Promises and Perils of Massive Open Online Courses.* Thanks to all of the folks who contributed chapters to that collection, many of whom also agreed to sit down with me for interviews for this book. Thanks to Elizabeth Losh and Kathleen Yancey for editing and publishing work about my early MOOC experiences and to the American Federation of Teachers and the Center for Academic Innovation at Creighton University for inviting me to speak about my MOOC scholarship in progress. Thanks also to Federica WebLearning at the Universitá di Napoli Federico II for inviting me to participate in their MOOC Conferences in Anacapri.

Finally, thanks to everyone at Utah State University Press, particularly Michael Spooner who took the initial chance on this project and to Rachael Levay who took the lead on bringing this project to its finish.

# MORE THAN A MOMENT

# INTRODUCTION

I am an accidental MOOC scholar.

My training, teaching, and scholarship are firmly rooted in composition and rhetoric. Pedagogy and distance education are key issues in the field, though we tend to approach these concerns differently than scholars who study education, particularly those interested in education policy or online pedagogy. I have taught writing courses online since 2005 but never courses that were "open" to anyone outside of my university. They were typically capped at twenty students, certainly never "massive."

So, how did I get here?

Well, the focus of both my teaching and scholarship has been the connection between writing and technology, and, following the lead of scholars like Walter Ong and Cynthia Selfe, I begin with the assumption that literacy itself is a technology. While my work has of course required computer hardware and software, and I identify myself as being in the loosely defined academic communities of "computers and writing" and "digital humanities," I also study older and now less novel technologies, especially as they pertain to the teaching of writing—pens, paper, chalkboards, correspondence courses, and so forth. This history has taught me that massive open online courses are a continuation of the instructional and distance education technologies that have been part of higher education since the late nineteenth century.

My interest and experience in online teaching (albeit in small, closed, credit-bearing online courses) piqued my curiosity about the emerging phenomenon of MOOCs. I enrolled as a MOOC student to get a view of just what was going on in these courses, blogging about a series of MOOCs, most actively in 2012–2013 but continuing today. Curiously, my blog writing about MOOCs was what solidified my standing as a "MOOC scholar." I wrote about my MOOC experiences, received positive feedback from readers, and wrote more. As I wrote more, I was approached to give presentations and to write journal articles about my experiences as a MOOC student. These opportunities and more blogging about MOOCs led to more positive feedback, and before I knew it, I was an expert.

DOI: 10.7330/9781607327875.c000

In March 2013, while attending the Conference for College Composition and Communication (the annual flagship academic meeting for composition and rhetoric scholars), I discussed the idea of an edited collection of essays about MOOCs with my colleague and ultimately co-editor Charles Lowe and the publisher of Parlor Press, David Blakesley. This was during the zenith of hype surrounding MOOCs in the academic and mainstream media, the height of the "MOOC moment." Among the thousands of writing scholars and teachers attending that year's conference in Las Vegas, there was a palpable fear that MOOCs were going to roll in and replace general education courses like first-year writing and that many of us were either going to be working for "the machine" or be out of a job entirely. The moment was right for a collection of essays, particularly a collection that approached MOOCs from the point of view of students, teachers, and scholars and decidedly *not* from the point of view of pundits, administrators, and entrepreneurs—that is, not from the point of view of the voices that had been most prominent in the media up to that point. The collection, *Invasion of the MOOCs: The Promises and Perils of Massive Open Online Courses*, was published in 2014, less than a year later. Through that project I connected with a number of faculty around the country who developed and taught MOOCs, particularly writing courses, and those connections led to interviews with faculty about their experiences developing and teaching MOOCs.

This journey into the realm of massive open online courses that began by chance a few years ago has led me here, to *More than a Moment*. Back in 2013 or so, the phrase "the MOOC moment" appeared in dozens (if not hundreds) of titles and headlines for presentations, blog posts, chapters, academic articles, and mainstream media pieces—certainly in part because of the words' alliterative qualities but also because the phrase neatly described for many observers what was happening. MOOCs appeared to come from nowhere and in an instant. Then, when MOOCs failed to transform higher education as we know it, the phrase "the MOOC moment" was rolled out in titles and headlines to note the temporary and past-tense status of MOOCs. The moment had passed.

*More than a Moment* argues that MOOCs were never an entirely new phenomenon and that MOOCs and their influences are far from over. This book explores the context around and within MOOCs, both in terms of the history of higher education that enabled MOOCs and also the situation within MOOCs themselves. The speed of the rise and fall of MOOCs was unprecedented, but the pattern is not. There have been numerous innovations and experiments in distance education over the past 150 or so years in American higher education, most of which promised to extend the opportunity to attend college to people who do not have the means or access to a traditional college education. These experiments have threatened the existing structure of higher education and have also emboldened education entrepreneurs focused on turning a profit. MOOCs and their futures demonstrate the ways higher education depends on centuries of tradition while simultaneously challenging the methods of delivery, the roles of students and instructors, and the shifting definition of "education" itself.

*More than a Moment* asks:

- Where did MOOCs come from, and how have they followed and deviated from the history of distance education technologies?
- What can we learn from the experiences of MOOC students and teachers about their future potential for both "learning" and "institutional education?"
- How can we learn from the MOOC phenomenon to recognize the opportunities and threats of future innovations in distance education and in partnerships between nonprofit institutions and for-profit educational entrepreneurs?

## WHERE I'M COMING FROM AS A COMPOSITION AND RHETORIC SCHOLAR IN SOUTHEAST MICHIGAN

Before I outline the chapters in *More than a Moment*, I want to describe my disciplinary background and my assumptions about what makes education work—specifically, what makes a system of institutional education different from a learning experience. I think it's important to do this because I am assuming an audience of readers who are educators, administrators, and entrepreneurs interested in distance education generally and MOOCs in particular but also readers who aren't necessarily familiar with my field, composition and rhetoric. Besides that disciplinary filter, my understanding and analysis of MOOCs are also shaped by my locale in terms of the university where I work and my assumptions about the required elements for what it takes for a system of institutional education to work.

When I tell people (and this includes academics in other disciplines) I'm a professor specializing in composition and rhetoric, they frequently ask "what's that?" I usually answer this question with another: "Do you remember freshman composition?" "Of course," most answer, since the experience of first-year writing is almost universal for Americans who were college students in the United States. And often enough, people then tell me the story of their first-year writing course as tremendously inspiring, tremendously awful, or, oddly, a bit of both.

While the "freshman comp" experience has been a part of higher education in the United States since the late nineteenth century, the academic specialization known as "composition and rhetoric" is comparatively new, not really emerging in full at the PhD level until the late 1970s–early 1980s, and it wasn't acknowledged as a distinct field (rather than a specialization within English studies) until the 1990s. Composition and rhetoric programs have been moving away from literary studies for some time now, and there has been an increase in recent years in free-standing writing programs and departments where the long-standing first-year writing course—often along with undergraduate majors and graduate programs in writing studies—are independent of an English department. The study of composition and rhetoric at the graduate level can be traced to first-year writing pedagogy, but the field has grown well beyond that. We teach and study about rhetoric, professional and technical writing, media studies, writing across the curriculum, and, of course, writing pedagogy designed to prepare future writing teachers. Further complicating matters (especially relative to MOOCs) is that composition and rhetoric as a discipline is primarily an American phenomenon: that is, while there is interest in writing studies around the world, the notion of a universal writing requirement at the first-year level and the study of the theory and pedagogy of writing in graduate school are almost completely unknown outside of the United States and Canada, and only a handful of universities outside the United States offer advanced undergraduate or graduate study in the field. So, while MOOCs are an international phenomenon, my discipline is not.

Broadly speaking, the widely assumed best practices in composition and rhetoric are at odds with the pedagogical approaches of MOOCs. Two often-repeated guiding principles in the field, which I will return to in the coming chapters, seem particularly at odds with the ways MOOCs work. The first is the "student-centered classroom." The ideal writing course should not be about the "sage on the stage" star lecturing professor depositing knowledge into listening students. Rather, the role of a writing teacher is to create and foster a classroom environment in which students are active in constructing their learning, and the students' writing projects are the primary texts of the course. The second closely related principle is "writing is a process," meaning writing is not a content area where knowledge can be delivered to students, nor is learning about writing merely a matter of producing the final product of writing—a grammatically correct (albeit boring and regurgitative) paper for the teacher to grade. Rather, learning to write is a social activity that depends on practicing and thinking about the steps in the writing process (such as brainstorming, drafting, research-ing, and revising based on feedback from others), and it also depends on teachers encouraging their students to engage with each others' writing processes with feedback and participation. These principles are closely related to the sort of critical pedagogy advocated by Paulo Freire, Ira Shor, and Henry Giroux (among many others, of course). To enable this pedagogy, writing courses are small, typically somewhere between fifteen and twenty-five students. The assumptions behind this approach, as Stephanie Odom and Leslie Lindsey write, are that "a low student-to-teacher ratio is critical because effective writing classes are not information-oriented or lecture-focused, but rather guided oppor-tunities for students to practice the writing process and receive appro-priate feedback." Odom and Lindsey (2016, 333) go on to say that the interaction and rapport between teachers and students in writing classes is necessary to effectively learn about writing.

Interestingly, because first-year writing is almost universally required of all college students in the United States, and it is not at all unusual for even medium-sized universities to offer dozens of twenty- to twenty-five-student sections of the course (my own university typically offers about sixty sections of first-year writing a term), it is cost-prohibitive to staff so many different sections with tenure-track faculty who are composition and rhetoric specialists. As a result, individual sections of first-year writ-ing end up being taught by graduate assistants and part-time and full-time (but not necessarily tenure-track) faculty who are not necessarily trained in the field. Tenure-track faculty who *are* specialists in composi-tion and rhetoric often act in the quasi-administrative role of "writing program administrator," loosely supervising and mentoring dozens of non-tenure-track instructors. The specifics of how this plays out at dif-ferent universities vary, but, generally speaking, these staffing practices make first-year writing courses "ground zero" in discussions about the reliance on disenfranchised teachers and otherwise non-tenure-track faculty in higher education today.

Because these and other guiding principles of my field are at odds with presumptions about how MOOCs work, I began my involvement with MOOCs as a skeptic. MOOCs involve thousands of students fol-lowing along closely the lectures of the "star" professor leading the course. *Maybe this could work for university courses that are taught in lecture hall formats now. But how,* I thought (presumably, just like most of my col-leagues in composition and rhetoric), *can you expect students to learn about writing in an environment like that?* As I think becomes clear throughout *More than a Moment,* I remain skeptical about the potential of MOOCs to *replace* what we do in small classes in first-year writing (and similar courses across academia). But it is useful to consider how MOOCs raise questions about the pedagogical presumptions most scholars in the field hold dear. For example, does the massiveness of MOOCs really impede the social and interactive process we believe is only possible in small writing courses? Can student peer review stand in for faculty feedback? Does assessment of student writing completed in MOOCs scale?

"Massiveness" aside, I did not begin this project with the same skepticism about the online nature of MOOCs. And just to be clear: MOOCs and online courses are not the same thing. I've been teaching a variety of advanced undergraduate and graduate writing courses online since 2005, and I think I've been able to teach them effectively. In my experience, small and closed (that is, courses only available to registered and tuition-paying students) online courses can be just as effective as face-to-face courses, with two important caveats. First, students need more experience, discipline, and self-motivation to succeed in online courses. The students I have had in my online classes who did not succeed often made the mistake of thinking the online class was going to somehow be easier than the face-to-face version. I often compare registering for an online class to registering for a gym membership—it only works if you actually go—and when students do not succeed in online classes, it is typically because they overestimated their abilities to stay self-motivated and disciplined about keeping up with an online class.

Second, it's not useful to compare online courses to face-to-face courses in terms of which is "better"; rather, the consideration should be about the *affordances* of these different forms of delivery. Online courses have the advantage of bending (though not necessarily eliminating) the specifics of meeting times and meeting spaces, while face-to-face courses have the advantage of being able to exchange a great deal of information between teachers and students efficiently. The point is this: I began this project with a lot of experience about how online teaching works; indeed, as I think will be clear in recapping the interviews I conducted with MOOC faculty, I began my time as a MOOC student with a lot more experience with online pedagogy than many faculty members who have been tasked with teaching MOOCs.

My perspectives on MOOCs are also a result of my experiences as an academic on the lower to middle end of the clear but unspoken hierarchy of higher education. David F. Labaree describes this non-organized order of things in the United States in his book *A Perfect Mess: The Unlikely Ascendancy of American Higher Education* (2017). Labaree's basic thesis is that many of the problems that continue to plague higher education in the United States—such as the debate about college being for the betterment of society and the pursuit of intellectual ideals versus being for an individual pursuit for a credential attractive to employers, the often-blurry lines between nonprofit and public entities and for-profit and private companies, and the inequalities among institutions—have been problems for well over 150 years. Further, much of the reason why most of the best universities in the world are in the United States is because of the institutions' relative autonomy from government control and their reliance on student tuition and alumni support. It's a book that is at times counterintuitive and paradoxical but always interesting and persuasive.

Labaree points out that in the United States, we "make universities both accessible and elite by creating a pyramid of institutions in which access is inclusive at the bottom and exclusive at the top." This current system, which both "extends opportunity" while it simultaneously "protects privilege," has created "a structure in which universities are formally equal but functionally quite different, where those institutions that are most accessible provide the least social benefit, and those that are the least accessible open the most doors" (Labaree 2017, 5). The accessible base of this pyramid emerged in the twentieth century from what were called "junior colleges" but are now known as community colleges. The next tier consists of universities that have largely evolved out of nineteenth-century "normal schools," which were originally established to prepare teachers for the increasing number of secondary schools (Labaree 2017, 11). Second from the top tier are the universities that emerged from the land-grant colleges that also came into place in the nineteenth century, institutions that expanded "access for a broader array of students and offer . . . programs with practical applications in areas like agriculture and engineering" (Labaree 2017, 10). At the top of the pyramid are Ivy League colleges that "emerged in the colonial period, followed by a series of flagship state colleges" and other elite research universities (Labaree 2017, 10). Interestingly, Labaree specifically brackets in a different category colleges and universities with an explicit religious mission because these are institutions that exist at all levels of his hierarchy, and he also does not include for-profit proprietary institutions in his system.

I live and work in a county where Labaree's academic pyramid is clear and obvious. I am a professor at what Labaree would categorize as a "third-tier" university, Eastern Michigan University. EMU has a few PhD programs and many master's degree programs, but we are mainly focused on undergraduate education. We're an "opportunity granting" institution in that many of our students come here because we accept over two-thirds of the students who apply, and we are affordable. We are a regional university, and almost all of our students are from southeast Michigan and the Detroit metropolitan area. About a third of our students are people of color, many of our students transfer here from area community colleges, and many are first-generation college students from lower-middle-class/working-class backgrounds. In other words, while I (mostly) love working at EMU for all kinds of different reasons, it's just one of 300 or so similar institutions in the United States, many of which are recognizable by the inclusion of a direction in their names. It is personally special to me because of my colleagues and my students, but statistically, it's not at all above average.

In contrast, EMU is 7 miles away from the main campus of the University of Michigan. The suburban sprawl between Ypsilanti and Ann Arbor is continuous, and the borders between the cities and townships are only clear to locals. Depending on your route from EMU's campus to UM's, you might pass by two other institutions in Labaree's hierarchy, Washtenaw Community College and Concordia University (which is associated with the Lutheran Church). Michigan is an elite research university, routinely ranked as one of the top twenty-five universities in the world, and it is one of the best public universities in the United States. It has about 29,000 undergraduates and 15,000 graduate students, and it is highly selective. The students are mostly white and upper middle class, and they come from all over the world. In fact, over half of the students attending the university aren't from the state of Michigan, and those out-of-state students pay about two-and-a-half times more than in-state students. And, of course, UM was one of the elite institutions MOOC providers partnered with from the beginning. In short, while EMU and UM are close to each other geographically, we are very, very far apart.

I mention all of this for two related reasons. First, institutions like my own—and not the elite schools that have partnered with the likes of edX and Coursera—have traditionally reached out to students who wouldn't otherwise have access to higher education because of an inadequate academic record from secondary school, because of the cost of attendance, because of the location of the institution, and so forth. While MOOCs have made the idea of online coursework palatable to elite institutions like UM, institutions like EMU have been offering online courses and programs for decades. In other words, institutions like EMU have long been doing what MOOC providers say they are trying to do in terms of "extending opportunity" to otherwise disenfranchised students.

Second, as I will discuss more in the closing chapter, if the future of MOOCs represents a potentially existential challenge to higher education as we know it, then it is institutions like mine that are the most vulnerable. Elite universities are in no danger from what is emerging after the MOOC moment or by any system of certificates or badges offered in lieu of a college degree. I predict that students in 2068 will still be attending UM in ways similar to the way they are attending the university today (albeit with different majors, modes of delivery, kinds of students, and so forth), and UM will still be considered one of the leading institutions in the world. I'm not as certain about the future of my own institution. If what comes after MOOCs gains traction in higher education in the future, will the EMUs of higher education continue to exist as the main institutional support for opportunity-seeking students?

## WHAT "LEARNING" AND "INSTITUTIONAL EDUCATION" MEAN TO ME

To understand the reasons why MOOCs failed within higher education but continue to succeed outside of it, it's important to parse through the differences between "learning" versus "institutional education." Perhaps this is common sense, but it's worthwhile to spell out these differences explicitly in my introduction because I will be referring to them throughout this book.

Learning is about gaining knowledge or skills, and we learn in lots of different ways—through play, practice, experience, experiments, and study. There are few required components necessary to enable a learning opportunity; all a learner needs is some motivation and desire and some kind of content. Sometimes, particularly in play, the content of learning is other learners or even imaginary; sometimes the content includes whatever is in our environment; and sometimes it includes some of the more formal delivery systems of content, things like books, television, film, the internet, and so forth. Learning doesn't have to involve a teacher, and all of us can think of things we've taught ourselves or learned with/from friends, but teachers (in the form of friends, peers, coaches, parents, and yes, actual teachers and professors) are often present so that they can make learning more efficient by virtue of both their advanced knowledge of whatever is being learned and also of their pedagogical approach.

I think humans are learning animals in that we need to learn things to survive, and we generally find learning pleasurable and fulfilling. Obviously, not everyone likes learning the same things, an assertion that's based on both my years of trying to teach writing to frequently resistant students and also my own dislike of learning things involving mathematics. But I do think people pursue learning simply because they enjoy and benefit from the experience. It's fun.

In contrast, institutional education is the formal schooling apparatus that enables the delivery of various kinds of evaluations, certificates, and degrees through a recognized, organized, and hierarchical bureaucracy. It's a technology characterized by specific roles for participants (e.g., students, teachers, professors, principals, deans) and where students are generally divided into groups based on both age and ability. Generally speaking, we divide institutional education in the United States into three groupings based on age and complexity: elementary, secondary, and higher. The division of students by age is particularly present in the early stages of institutional education, where "grades" of elementary students (first grade, second grade, and so forth) are based on the age of students rather than their specific abilities. These divisions shift toward complexity and ability as students advance through institutional education and particularly in higher education, but first-year college students still tend to be younger than fourth-year students, who tend to be younger than graduate students. In this country, children are required to participate in the institutional education system (and in most US states, those who opt out with an alternative, like home schooling, need to notify the government of this decision), at least through the middle of secondary education, better known as high school; and around 80 percent of Americans today graduate with a high school diploma. While that means that a significant 20 percent or so of Americans drop out of high school, the graduation rate from high school has made remarkable progress since the early twentieth century—in 1909 less than 20 percent of the US population graduated from high school (Bidwell 2015).

In the United States there are a variety of public, private, and for-profit institutions that fall generally into the category of "higher education." In addition to the unspoken hierarchies described by Labaree, there is also the more codified Carnegie Classification of Institutions of Higher Education. This system, developed by the Carnegie Commission on Higher Education and in place since 1970, has seven categories of institutions, with many divisions within those categories. For example, Washtenaw Community College is in the category "Associate's Colleges: Mixed Transfer/Career and Technical-High Nontraditional," and EMU was recently reclassified into the category "Doctoral Universities: Moderate Research Activity." The certifications or "degrees" students receive from higher education institutions are similar and widely recognizable in the culture by other colleges and universities, employers, the government, and citizens: that is, a bachelor's degree from EMU in a particular subject area is the same kind of credential as a bachelor's degree in a comparable subject area from UM or any other recognized university. Further, these degrees and their credits are transferable in different ways. For example, while there are always specific institutional constraints, it is possible for students to take courses at EMU and then transfer them to a different degree program at UM, and vice versa. And while the somewhat arbitrary cultural value of a bachelor's degree from EMU is probably less than a bachelor's degree from UM in a similar field, both credentials would be sufficient for meeting the requirements of applying to graduate school or a particular job requiring that applicants have a college degree.

Institutional education at all levels is regulated by the government, particularly at primary and secondary levels. In fact, many primary and secondary school educators have argued that there is an overemphasis on this regulation in the form of being required to "teach to the test." Local school boards and community members frequently intervene down to the level of specific curricular choices, particularly in the case of controversial topics (sex education and the teaching of evolution immediately come to mind). While there are currently no mandated examinations for students in higher education analogous to what has been happening for decades in primary and secondary education, higher education institutions are also regularly reviewed by officially recognized and government-sanctioned accreditation bodies. Essentially, accreditors assure that the degrees offered by a particular institution are in line with that accreditor's standards, that the curriculum is sound, and that the institution falls into the realms of normal practices for the type of institution in question. Among many other things, universities need to be accredited for their students to be eligible for federal student aid and loan programs, and losing accreditation is usually the beginning of the end for that institution.

The point I'm belaboring here is that learning and institutional education are not the same thing. Learning and institutional education overlap like a Venn diagram, and every educator I've ever interacted with values learning and is also often frustrated with the aspects of institutional education that don't necessarily have much to do with learning. It is difficult to disagree with Sean Michael Harris and Jesse Stommel's (2017, 179) critique that too often institutional education is too engaged in the apparatus of delivering instruction based on particular outcomes and assessments: "Pedagogy, on the other hand, starts with learning as

its center, not students or teachers, and the work of pedagogues is necessarily political, subjective, and humane." At the same time, learning
alone is not enough for institutional education to continue to function.

A specific example of this frustration is grading. I have never met an
educator at any level who enjoys grading, and this is particularly true
in my field where grading is time-consuming and usually requires an
instructor to read and comment on hundreds of pages of student writing. Even in fields where evaluation and grading are more automated,
grading is usually seen as an unwelcome but necessary by-product of the
labor of teaching. At the same time, evaluating student performance in
courses is critical to the credentialing function of institutional education. When we speak of college students as "customers" (a highly problematic metaphor, of course), we're fundamentally talking about how
they are paying for the commodity of a degree, and that commodity
is made possible in large part because of assessment and grading. An
instructor's grade for a student is her certification regarding that specific course; when students gather enough of these certifications in the
form of passing grades in courses from a set curriculum (majors, minors,
general education) and earn enough credit hours from those courses,
the institution grants the student the appropriate and widely recognized
degree. Students would probably not enroll in courses or at universities
where they didn't feel they were learning anything, but they certainly
would not *pay* for those courses if there was no credit toward a degree
associated with them.

Many critics have argued that educational credentials are a waste of
time and money, that we ought to not require a bachelor's degree almost
universally for white-collar jobs, and that we ought to have an alternative system of training outside of systematized higher education. I have
sympathy with some of these critiques. But besides the fact that these
critics themselves have college degrees (and often advanced degrees
from elite universities) and that changing this reality would involve per-
suading employers who now require a college degree to reverse those
practices, I like to think that there is value in the credentialing offered
by institutional education. As an educator, I'm biased. But I'd argue that
the employee who is required to earn a college degree to get her job is
likely a better employee as a result of learning some things while passing
through the system of institutional education. Further, I go through my
day-to-day life reassured that the bureaucracy of institutional education
trained, assessed, and credentialed my physicians and nurses, my lawyer,
the engineers who helped design the car I drive, the scientists who helped
develop the medications I take, and the teachers who educate my child.

So, how do MOOCs—both as they exist now and as they are likely to exist in the near future—problematize this relationship between learning and institutional education? Can MOOCs and their progeny provide a learning environment that is a noticeable improvement over other learning delivery systems, things like television, radio, films, or books? Can something like MOOCs ever become a credible tool in terms of granting the credentials of institutional education, credentials that are compatible with (or an alternative to) traditional colleges and universities? Will learning and institutional education change because of innovations beyond MOOCs, or will entrenched assumptions about learning and institutional education end up limiting future possibilities?

OUTLINE

This book's first chapter, "MOOCs in the University Context: The Rapid Rise, Fall, and Failure of MOOCs in Higher Education," offers an overview of the meteoric rise and fall of massive open online courses. I describe their beginnings as a relatively limited Canadian experiment in hybrid face-to-face and online teaching to their swift rise as a threat to the ongoing existence of universities and higher education, which was just as swiftly followed by their dramatic fall. I outline this trajectory and then offer my explanation as to the ways MOOCs proved to be ineffective as a way of delivering institutional education.

Chapter 2, "MOOCs as a Continuation of Distance Education Technologies," is a selective history of some of the key innovations in distance education that preceded MOOCs: correspondence study of the late nineteenth and early twentieth centuries, radio and television courses in the middle of the twentieth century, and the first wave of online courses and degree programs in the late twentieth century. Despite the claims from MOOC entrepreneurs and enthusiastic media pundits, MOOCs are not entirely "new"; rather, MOOCs emerged from these distance education technologies, all of which either continue as an accepted means of delivering higher education or, in the case of public radio and television, have found relevance beyond institutional education.

Following the historical overview of these two chapters, I shift to an analysis of the contexts within MOOCs. Chapter 3, "MOOCs in the Student Context," is about my own experiences as a student, beginning with my active enrollment and participation in MOOCs in 2012 and concluding with my most recent (albeit incomplete) MOOC studies in 2017. This is followed by chapter 4, "MOOCs in the Faculty Context," which is based on interviews I conducted in 2015 with faculty and graduate assistants involved in the development and teaching of six different MOOCs. The faculty perspectives here are importantly different from those of those MOOC enthusiasts who tend to be administrators or entrepreneurs, and I also think these interviews say a lot about teaching practices in more conventional university settings too.

I conclude with "The Present and (Fuzzy and Difficult to Predict) Future of MOOCs and Beyond." As that mouthful of a chapter title suggests, I qualify my predictions of what's next because too many predictions of the inevitability of MOOCs disrupting higher education have been spectacularly wrong. Still, I am willing to predict that the future of MOOCs will continue to be important, particularly outside of higher education. The concerns and fears of MOOCs that preoccupied many academics from about 2012 to 2014 have passed. But the increasing role of Online Program Management companies in the marketing, development, and delivery of distance education threatens to make the distinction between nonprofit universities and for-profit educational companies even more complicated.

# 1

# MOOCS IN THE UNIVERSITY CONTEXT
## The Rapid Rise, Fall, and Failure of MOOCs in Higher Education

This chapter provides a broad overview of massive open online courses: how they came to pass and how they evolved, their rapid rise followed by an almost as rapid decline, and why MOOCs failed to change institutional education, particularly at the collegiate level. In a sense, this chapter recaps the recent and brief history of MOOCs seemingly coming out of nowhere as a threat to higher education around the world, only to be just as quickly dismissed as irrelevant. But as I hope becomes apparent with this and subsequent chapters, MOOCs and what has come out of the initial MOOC moment continue to be important.

## WHAT IS A MOOC?

Most readers interested in a book with a title like *More than a Moment: Contextualizing the Past, Present, and Future of MOOCs* are probably already familiar with the basics of massive open online courses. Since this project as a whole is trying to define MOOCs by tracing and describing the ways they have changed since the term was first coined, it's not easy to offer a complete and brief definition of MOOCs in a few pithy sentences. But, in the interest of introductions, I will describe MOOCs in broad terms and outline some of the basic points of contention around them.

The first online course to be called a MOOC was the 2008 course "Connectivism and Connective Knowledge," led/taught by Canadians George Siemens (then at Athabasca University) and Stephen Downes of Canada's National Research Council. Credit for actually coining the term *MOOC* goes to Dave Cormier, also a Canadian educator at the University of Prince Edward Island. The course, also known as CCK08, began as a group of about 25 tuition-paying students taking it through an extended education program at the University of Manitoba. Siemens and his colleagues opened the course to anyone interested, and about 2,200 online students took them up on their offer. It was, as Downes

DOI: 10.7330/9781607327875.c001

said, "evident early on that we had latched onto something when we got 100 times more participants in our course than we expected" (cited in Parr 2013).

In 2011, Stanford's Peter Norvig and Sebastian Thrun imitated/appropriated the MOOC concept and offered a course in artificial intelligence to 175 traditional students on campus and, simultaneously, to "over 100,000 via an interactive webcast" (Norvig 2012). By early 2012, Thrun had started one of the first large MOOC providers, Udacity, and fellow Stanford faculty Daphne Koller and Andrew Ng had started Coursera. edX, a partnership between Harvard University and MIT, was also founded in 2012. It's probably no wonder then that the *New York Times* declared in an often cited article that 2012 was "the Year of the MOOC" (Pappano 2012).

Siemens and Downes—particularly Downes—have had harsh words to say about the direction MOOCs have been taken by the large and for-profit MOOC providers. In a presentation at EDUCAUSE (which he shared on his website), Siemens (2012a) lamented that these MOOC providers seem to think they have "discovered" MOOCs, akin to a European explorer "discovering" America all over again. In a 2013 article in the *Times Higher Education*, Downes described the offerings from Coursera and the like as "unimaginative, created by people who for the most part are not aware of the history of online learning . . . The idea of MOOCs as an experiment in pedagogy and educational organization has been completely abandoned by the new platforms" (cited in Parr 2013).

In an effort to distinguish these different approaches to MOOCs, Siemens coined the terms *cMOOCs* and *xMOOCs*. This is how he described these different approaches to MOOCs on his blog: "Our MOOC model [the cMOOC] emphasizes creation, creativity, autonomy, and social networked learning. The Coursera model emphasizes a more traditional learning approach through video presentations and short quizzes and testing. Put another way, cMOOCs focus on knowledge creation and generation whereas xMOOCs focus on knowledge duplication. I've spoken with learners from different parts of the world who find xMOOCs extremely beneficial as they don't have access to learning materials of that quality at their institutions. xMOOCs scale, they have prestigious universities supporting them, and they are well-funded" (Siemens 2012a).

I am not fond of the terminology of cMOOC versus xMOOC, and, as I will discuss later in this chapter, I disagree with Siemens about the scalability of MOOCs. But I agree with the general distinction between

MOOCs offered as community-oriented and generative experiments versus MOOCs offered as imitations of lecture hall courses. I also have sympathy with the frustration evident in at least some of the statements on the state of MOOCs from Downes and Siemens. After all, what MOOCs became in the hands of venture-capitalist–funded entities like Coursera was not at all what their originators had in mind.

So, I initially define MOOCs as *massive open online courses offered initially as educational experiments and taken up by a variety of for-profit and not-for-profit entities and institutional collaborations in an effort to provide learning experiences to anyone with internet connectivity*. But each of the terms that make up the acronym "MOOC" is contentious, debatable, and evolving. These courses are "massive," though the range of participants is in the thousands to tens to hundreds of thousands, and as MOOCs shift to courses offered on individual demand with little interaction with other student participants, the sense of massiveness is largely absent. There are still a few "open" MOOCs where students can participate for free, but the vast majority of MOOCs now only provide certification or support to students (for example, a direct response to a student question from a course support staff member) for a fee. Besides, the large and corporate-supported MOOCs have never been truly "open" in the sense of "open education" or of creative commons licensing for content. Rather, MOOC providers have always struck complicated arrangements with publishers and other content providers, often limiting the availability of MOOC content after the conclusion of the course. MOOCs are still "online," though MOOC providers deliver their courses within the confines of their specific course management systems, and most MOOCs do not actively encourage the kind of multiple platform engagements that were a major part of the original MOOC experiments.

Even the acronym itself is changing. As the collection edited by Elizabeth Losh (2017), *MOOCs and Their Afterlives*, makes clear, the MOOC moment has spawned some changes to the original (massive open online *community* and massive open online *collaboration*) and some entirely different riffs on MOOCs, as in SPOCs (small private online courses), DOCCs (distributed online collaborative courses), and CLMOOCs (connected learning massive open online collaboration), just to name a few.

## THE RAPID RISE AND FALL OF MOOCS IN HIGHER EDUCATION

Despite the claims of MOOC entrepreneurs, MOOCs were not "new"; rather, they emerged out of a long tradition of experiments in American higher education (within both nonprofit universities and for-profit proprietary schools) with distance education. But one aspect of the "MOOC moment" that is unprecedented is the speed of their rise and fall. This is the aspect of MOOCs that has garnered most of the media attention in both the mainstream and education press, and it is also what first piqued my interest enough to enroll in MOOCs. Within the culture of higher education, where universities frequently trace their origins back centuries and it can take years for even the simplest change to work its way through the institutional bureaucracy, the fact that the rise and fall of MOOCs as a disruptive force has taken place in less than a decade is "unusual," to say the least.

The strategies of the large for-profit MOOC providers have always been a bit of a moving target and have varied from company to company, but in the beginning, Coursera and Udacity (and other MOOC providers) were attempting to provide a cheaper alternative to college degrees along with inexpensive course credits that could be taken as an alternative to or as part of a more traditional bachelor's degree. In other words, MOOC providers first thought the students/customers most interested in their courses would be similar to traditional undergraduates, including potential students outside of the United States who lacked access to higher education for various reasons. Udacity's founder Sebastian Thrun hyperbolically, albeit vaguely, predicted a future where there "will be only 10 institutions in the world delivering higher education and Udacity has a shot at being one of them" (cited in Leckart 2012).

Coursera's Daphne Koller was somewhat more specific. In June 2012 at TEDGlobal, Koller gave a popular talk (one that has been viewed over 2.3 million times) in which she outlined the vision of what she hoped Coursera might become: an opportunity to bring the world's best professors and scholars and a high-quality college education to the disenfranchised all over the world. She began her talk by describing her own educational privilege as a third-generation PhD and how lucky she was to have had such access to higher education. Then she shifted to a moving anecdote about the lack of access to higher education in countries like South Africa where a crowd of thousands hoping to win one of the last admission spots to the University of Johannesburg stampeded, ultimately injuring twenty and "one woman died. She was a mother who gave her life trying to get her son a chance at a better life" (Koller 2012). Along with what I presume is a sincere philanthropic mission, Koller and her partners at Coursera also had the beginnings of a money-making strategy that included what Koller described in an interview with

Kevin Carey (2016, 155) as a "blue ocean" business: "If only two percent of all of the people in the world are willing to pay $74 for a service" like a Coursera course certificate, "that's $10 billion a year, which is a lot of revenue for a company that can fit all of its employees into one part of one floor of a commercial office building in Palo Alto." There were plenty of investors who believed in these predictions and strategies, too; by the middle of 2012, Coursera had raised at least $20 million in venture capital, and Udacity was not far behind.

Because MOOC providers lacked content and establishment cache, they convinced major universities that they needed to partner with the new MOOC upstarts to remain one of those ten or so universities Thrun predicted would be left in a few decades. Many universities made these deals eagerly because of some combination of similarly altruistic motivations about extending educational opportunities, because they thought Coursera and Udacity might very well threaten their long-term existence, and because of the classic Silicon Valley venture-capitalist "Fear of Missing Out" (FOMO). As Ian Bogost (2017, 271) put it (perhaps a bit too cynically), "MOOCs allow academic institutions to signal that they are with-it and progressive, in tune with the contemporary technological climate."

By July 2012, Coursera was already beginning to pivot toward revenue resources beyond the blue ocean of would-be college students. In an analysis of the contract between Coursera and the University of Michigan, Jeffrey R. Young noted that ideas for revenue included selling certificates (which might or might not be transferable into college credit), employer or university screening and recruiting, corporate training, and advertising. Not everyone was optimistic about these plans. Higher education analyst Trace A. Urdan told Young (2012) he found it "'ironic' that major universities are embracing online education when they have been dismissive of earlier efforts by for-profit companies like the University of Phoenix." Urdan went on: "These are two of the most arrogant types of institutions—Silicon Valley companies intersecting with these elite academic programs. Neither of them considers that anyone else [had] come to this place before they've arrived. They say, 'We're here now, so now it's sort of legitimate and for real'" (Young 2012).

Still, MOOC enthusiasm continued. Several states (including New York and California) floated proposals exploring how MOOC courses and credits could be used to help students in their public university systems make better progress toward completing their degrees. In November 2012, the Bill and Melinda Gates Foundation added fuel to this fire by announcing "12 grants, totaling more than $3 million, in new investments in MOOCs." A little over half of a million dollars of these grants was directed toward institutions developing "introductory and remedial level MOOCs," including four institutions working on MOOCs in writing: Mt. San Jacinto College, Georgia Tech, Ohio State University, and Duke University (Bill and Melinda Gates Foundation 2012). As you will see in chapters 3 and 4, I enrolled in and write about my experiences participating in one of those MOOCs, Duke's "English Composition 1: Achieving Expertise." I also interviewed some of the writing MOOC faculty from Georgia Tech, Ohio State, and Duke who won these Gates Foundation grants and developed these courses.

In January 2013, Coursera announced its "verified certificate" program in which students pay an upfront fee (the exact amount varied, but it was typically somewhere around $50–$125) and agree to have their identity verified by webcam and typing patterns (Young 2013). San Jose State and MOOC provider Udacity also announced a pilot program for offering a series of remedial and introductory courses in subjects like algebra in online and blended/hybrid class formats.

By March 2013, the hallway talk at the Conference for College Composition and Communication (the flagship convention for my field, held that year in Las Vegas) was about MOOCs. The more scholarly discussion about MOOCs wouldn't catch up with current events until the following year's conference, when there were nearly forty presentations on the program about MOOCs, but the media hype about MOOCs manifested itself as an uneasy fear at the 2013 conference. After all, most of those attending derived their livelihood by teaching and administering the kinds of courses and programs that might very well be replaced by MOOCs. It was also at that conference where my co-editor Charles Lowe and I began soliciting interest in contributions to the collection *Invasion of the MOOCs*, which was well under way by summer 2013.

But by mid-2013, the enthusiasm for MOOCs as a disruptive force in higher education began to fade. It had been apparent long before then that the completion rates for MOOCs were abysmal, and most of the students enrolled already held a bachelor's degree and thus had no interest in or need for paying for undergraduate college credit. In July 2013, the *Chronicle of Higher Education* reported on a MOOC offered through Colorado State University–Global Campus—the first MOOC that would have granted college credit to students who completed the computer science course and paid $89 for the required proctored final exam—in which no students took CSU up on the offer to pay for credit (Kolowich 2013). The Udacity MOOC partnership with San Jose State was "paused" after results from the spring 2013 version of the MOOC demonstrated that students did "not fare as well as students who attended normal classes" (Rivard 2013). In fact, "The failure rates in the five [Udacity MOOCs] ranged from 56 to 76 percent. Nor was the course material exactly rocket science—the five classes were in elementary statistics, college algebra, entry-level math, introduction to programming, and introduction to psychology" (Oremus 2013). A few months later, Thrun made a 180 degree turn on his earlier prediction regarding Udacity's future place among the great universities of the world, admitting in a *Fast Company* interview, "we have a lousy product" (Chafkin 2013).

The bold plans Coursera's Daphne Koller offered in a 2012 TED talk to bypass the established system of higher education and bring education to the disenfranchised masses were also tempered by the realities of the outcomes. In a 2015 interview, Koller acknowledged the "disillusionment" that accompanied the MOOC hype. Coursera was shifting its target audience from disenfranchised students seeking college degrees to "people who are primarily working adults and are not currently candidates for traditional forms of education," and it shifted to offering certificates for courses or a set of courses—for a fee, of course: "Coursera is currently the second biggest credential supplier on LinkedIn, right after Microsoft, which is incredible since we've only been operating for about 2.5 years. This suggests that prospective employees are seeing value in the credentials" ("The Hype Is Dead, but MOOCs Are Marching On" 2015). This has proven to be a relatively successful pivot, though certainly a far cry from the promises and visions the company had just a few years earlier.

Soon after this fall, the entrepreneurs originally behind Coursera and Udacity moved on. Coursera co-founder Andrew Ng left in 2014, and Koller left in 2016. Also in 2016, Sebastian Thrun stepped down as CEO of Udacity, though he continues to work full-time at the MOOC provider he started in "a role focused on what he is passionate about—innovation" (Rao 2016). In an October 2017 interview published in India, Udacity vice president Clarissa Shen said "MOOCs are dead," and the company was moving away from them (Khosla 2017). Shen walked this claim back a bit in a different October 2017 interview in *EdSurge*, saying she was not suggesting a "new strategy" for the company and that there was still a lot of free content available (Young 2017). Nonetheless, Shen's insider appraisal of the status of MOOCs in 2017 was perhaps more honest and accurate than she intended.

## HOW AND WHY MOOCS "FAILED" IN
## INSTITUTIONAL EDUCATION (SO FAR)

While the existential threat of massive open online courses replacing colleges and universities has ended, MOOCs still exist and are still relevant. There is still a lot to be learned from the ways MOOCs followed and diverged from the history of previous innovations in instructional technology and also from the student and teacher experience within MOOCs. As I will discuss in the last chapter, the MOOC moment is not actually over, and institutional education continues to be impacted by its aftermath. MOOCs continue to grow in terms of the number of offerings; in partnerships with universities, corporations, and institutions; and also in terms of the number of people enrolling. MOOCs have progressed outside of academia, and they also continue to influence traditional assumptions about online education and the complex relationships between nonprofit universities and for-profit educational services companies.

As "learning opportunities," MOOCs worked and continue to work. I certainly learned from the MOOCs I took. But MOOCs failed as a means of delivering institutional education; that is, they failed to disrupt the way universities teach students (especially undergraduates) and award degrees. There are a lot of reasons for this. I will focus here on three broad and overlapping reasons for this failure.

*While Content "Scales," Institutional Education and*
*Assessment Do Not (At Least Not Well Enough)*

By "scale," I mean the way the term is employed in the business and technology sector regarding growth. The ideally scalable business is one in which adding customers or users does not significantly increase the operating costs of providing the product or service. Content—particularly when it's made available as a website or a document available for download—is very scalable. If I publish a website or post a document that users can download, the costs of making that content available are not significantly different if only 1 user downloads the document or if 100,000 users do.

MOOC providers (like many entrepreneurs in the education market) assumed that institutional education is primarily about delivering content. This misinterpretation is perhaps understandable because there is a lot of content in institutional education. The heart of any university is its library, which is a repository of content. Courses are loaded with content in the form of textbooks, articles, tests, quizzes, and writing assignments. But if institutional education were the same thing as content, then the need for schools and universities would have ended with the development of literacy thousands of years ago.

I do qualify this a bit by saying that institutional education does not scale "well enough" because some kinds of courses and subject areas work better than others in the MOOC environment. Course subjects that universities are confident offering in larger sections or in lecture hall settings are more scalable than the courses colleges and universities are more confident and comfortable offering in smaller discussion or seminar-sized class settings. The large lecture hall is never the ideal classroom setting for any subject, which is why one of the most common marketing claims traditional universities and colleges make is to highlight a low student-to-instructor ratio. Nonetheless, higher education has been comfortable with offering courses in lecture hall formats of 100 to 500 students (though less comfortable with lecture hall courses the size of even the smallest MOOCs) when those courses are content-driven and the assessment process is based on straightforward and quantitative tests and quizzes—for example, introductory courses in the sciences and computer programming. But when the primary purpose of the course is the discussion of ideas and the assessment is based on qualitative writing tasks and presentations, then courses need to be smaller. First-year composition and rhetoric immediately comes to mind, but smaller course sizes are common across the humanities for similar reasons.

But again, the value of institutional education for the broader culture and the workplace is not exclusively content. You don't need to be enrolled in an organic chemistry class to read an organic chemistry textbook. Rather, the value comes from interacting with other students and with teachers, the assessment of tests and other assignments by experts, and, of course, the earned degree that comes from completing a prescribed series of courses.

Kevin Carey predicted the collapse of higher education because of skyrocketing costs and alternatives to college degrees resulting from developments in instructional technology (including MOOCs). Among many other things, Carey argues against the value of higher education degrees and credentials. A credential "is just information," he writes. "Like modern financial currency, the value of that information is nothing more than what people collectively attribute to it" (Carey 2016, 186). He complains that there is little information in the credential itself, comparing degrees and transcripts to the minimalistic level of detail "captured prisoners of war are required to disclose under the Geneva Conventions: name, rank, and serial number (or academic major)"

(Carey 2016, 197). And yet, the societal agreement on the value of a college degree is incredibly important, at least as important as the social/cultural/legal agreement we have about the symbolic value of recognized currency—which is why Bitcoin and similar alternatives to financial currency are still considered high-risk investments.

We need to have regulatory authority regarding college credentials and degrees. "A free-form market economy in non-standardized credentials would only lead to predatory and deceptive practices," Karen Head (2017, 60) writes in her book about her MOOC experiences. "This was one reason that the New York State attorney general required the online Trump 'University' to stop advertising itself as a university." As I wrote in the introduction, students might or might not enroll in universities if they felt they weren't going to learn anything, but they would certainly not enroll in universities if the degree offered after a course of study had no cultural or employment value. Rebecca Bennett and Mike Kent (2017, 20) summarize this argument well: "Revolutionary narratives about MOOCs were based on the premise that knowledge alone is power. However, in a stratified, institutionalised global education system, the power of knowledge is measured by certification. The issue with learning for learning's sake is that there is no recognisable evidence that knowledge has been acquired, tested or verified. Universities are in place to offer institutionally verified certification of knowledge acquisition—the most powerful and globally recognised form of this knowledge is a bachelor's degree."

Of course, institutional education goes far beyond assessment: we help students learn more effectively. Professors and teachers help students navigate the material, answer questions, foster the kinds of discussions in classes that generate knowledge and learning. We motivate, persuade, and advise students about their studies through a complex mix of rewards and punishments. The work of institutional education goes beyond faculty in the classroom, too: all sorts of academic and nonacademic staff at institutions, from librarians and tutors and administrators to the staff working in the dorms, the cafeterias, and other areas more generally labeled "student life," are involved in the process. Students in a community of other students are also an enormous part of the value of institutional education. They help each other learn, they give each other a sense of community and identity, and fellow students are an extremely important source of social and personal growth, particularly for traditional college students in their late teens and early twenties. I know no one who was a traditional college student who was not profoundly shaped by the experience and has not maintained at least some connection with past classmates and institutions even decades later.

Universities are not 100 percent successful, and, to the extent that graduation rates are one measure of a university's ability to deliver institutional education, it's clear that some institutions are better than others. But it is the entire apparatus of institutional education—not just its content—that makes the system work. Focusing on content and minimizing the costliest part of education, the labor force that does everything to make the system work, does not scale.

### MOOC Providers (and Pundits) Severely Underestimated Both the Historical Depth and Breadth of Higher Education

The original MOOC entrepreneurs were fond of claiming that nothing has changed in higher education for hundreds of years—that is, until MOOCs came along. This same circle of critics often argues that higher education as an "industry" is on the brink of failure. I've mentioned Thrun's famous prediction of the future success of Udacity. Head analyzes in detail the "disruption genre" as it applies to higher education and MOOCs, particularly of the books *The Innovative University: Changing the DNA of Higher Education from the Inside Out* by Clayton Christensen and Henry Eyring, and *Abelard to Apple: The Fate of American Colleges and Universities* by Richard DeMillo. As recently as November 2017, CNBC reported Christensen repeating his 2011 prediction that half of the 4,000 or so institutions that make up higher education in the United States would be bankrupt in ten or fifteen years (Hess 2017). Christensen also predicted that by 2019, "half of all classes for grades K–12 will be taught online" (obviously, the window regarding the accuracy of that prediction has closed) (Myers 2011). Carnegie Mellon Provost Emeritus Mark S. Kamlet told Carey in an interview that the twentieth-century expansion of higher education was coming to an end, and only a few universities—maybe fifteen, maybe twenty-five, maybe fifty—would survive into the coming future (Carey 2016, 72). Former Stanford president John L. Hennessy predicted in 2012 that a "tsunami" of dramatic change was coming to higher education in the form of online courses and MOOCs (Jaschik 2015). And so forth.

But these same predictors of disruption and the demise of universities never seem to explore the question of how these supposedly stagnant and backward-thinking institutions have stayed open and continued to grow and enroll students for hundreds of years. In other words, if higher education is unable to both innovate and persist, if higher education truly is vulnerable to the same kind of market forces that ruined other content-heavy industries like print journalism, then why are so many old universities still in business with students eager to attend them?

There have been many failures in higher education along the way, obviously. David Labaree (2017) notes that many of the colleges created in the United States—particularly in the nineteenth century—long ago either closed or merged with other institutions. It is also true that there are undeniable strains and problems in higher education in the United States. Cathy N. Davidson (2017a) makes clear that MOOCs are not what has created these problems, nor are they the solution. "Our adjunct crisis, our overstuffed lecture halls . . . our crushing faculty workloads" and the exponential rise in student tuition have been problems that have resulted from "fifty years of neoliberalism, including the actual defunding of public higher education by state legislatures" (Losh 2017, 71). So, the predictions of the decline of higher education in the United States and throughout the world should not be ignored because there are indeed serious problems and threats. Christensen and his ilk are grossly exaggerating the problems in higher education today, but it's hard to deny that there are problems.

At the same time, those who argue that higher education will collapse because of a lack of innovation—particularly as these predictions pertain to MOOCs as a solution to the problems—are ignoring the status of higher education around the globe and in the United States, and the best evidence of higher education's deep establishment is its long history. Labaree, quoting from a 1983 Clark Kerr study, notes that about eighty-five institutions were established in the Western world by 1520 and have continually existed in similar, albeit evolved, ways. These institutions include the Catholic Church, Parliaments in Great Britain and Iceland, and about seventy universities (Labaree 2017, 3). All of the top twenty-five universities in the world (as ranked by the *Times Higher Education*) are at least 100 years old, and most are much older than that (Oxford was founded almost 1,000 years ago, Harvard was founded in 1636, and even comparable new kids on the block Cal Tech and Stanford were founded in the 1890s). Even most of the universities that fall in the "third tier" of Labaree's hierarchy of higher education in the United States—places like Eastern Michigan University—trace their roots back to the mid-nineteenth century (EMU was founded in 1849). As Labaree also makes clear throughout his book, these very old colleges and universities are even more important in the United States today on both the top and bottom of the hierarchy. The top schools (which also tend to be the oldest universities) continue to enjoy increasing student interest and alumni contributions to their endowments. At the same time, the lower-tier schools continue because of the need for a college degree for most middle-class and white-collar jobs. In short, higher education is not an "industry" like print journalism or similar industries vulnerable to technological innovation; the established and entrenched status of higher education makes it more analogous to the Catholic Church and the world's oldest democracies.

I also think MOOC entrepreneurs didn't understand the *breadth* of higher education that exists in the United States. The founders of the major MOOC providers were all products of the most elite of the elite higher education institutions in this country, and the universities they partnered with to develop MOOC courses were also in that category of elite and selective universities. They believed MOOCs were a way of extending access to an educational experience to the masses who didn't have access to their elite universities. But these MOOC providers ignored the vast majority of institutions at the base of the pyramid of the higher education hierarchy described by Labaree: the community colleges and third-tier/regional universities and colleges that provide extensive access to higher education in this country. Labaree (2017, 159–160) writes: "Out of the 4,700 institutions of higher education in the United States, only 191 are selective in admissions, meaning that they accept fewer than half of the students who apply. That's only 4 percent; 96 percent of American colleges accept most applicants."

In other words, MOOC entrepreneurs somehow missed the deep cultural entrenchment of higher education. They also somehow missed the fact that higher education's long history and slow change probably meant it has been doing something right, and they forgot that education was already being brought to the masses in the United States by community colleges and regional universities. As Matt Reed (2015) pointed out in his critique of Arizona State University's Global Freshman Academy (I'll discuss my GFA experience in chapter 3), community colleges can offer a better learning experience than a MOOC and courses that can reliably be transferred to a college or a university toward a bachelor's degree or applied toward an established associates degree, and they can do this for less money. It is no wonder that the GFA has seen so little interest from MOOC students to pay for actual college credit.

*MOOC Providers Fundamentally Misunderstood the Students/*
*Customers Who Would Want Their Courses/Product*

As I learned from my own early experiences as a MOOC student and in the interviews I conducted with MOOC faculty and developers, MOOC providers assumed that the people most interested in their courses would be similar to traditional college students—specifically, the kinds of traditional college students these MOOC developers were used to encountering in their courses and institutions. These assumptions were wrong in at least two fundamental ways.

First, as Bennett and Kent (2017, 17) describe it, early MOOC developers mistakenly assumed that their MOOC students would be like their own students and colleagues at elite universities: "This is not necessarily intentional but it is based on the assumption that every student experience is similar to the experiences of the course designer. For example, [Jeffrey] Selingo cites MOOC founder Sebastian Thrun attesting to this failing in his initial course design when he realised he was using the same pedagogy for MOOCs as he used for classes designed for his elite students at Stanford: 'The basic MOOC is a great thing for the top five percent of the student body, but not a great thing for the bottom ninety-five percent.'" Cathy Davidson (2017b, 122) is more blunt: "The San Jose State experiment"—that is, the Udacity MOOC that failed and which prompted Thrun's "we have a lousy product" quote—"exposed the fantasy that technology will 'make' learning easy. It won't. That's just not how learning works."

Second, MOOC providers initially made some wrong assumptions about what those who enrolled in their MOOCs wanted out of the experience. MOOCs were first developed with traditional first-year college students in mind, but the majority of students who registered for MOOCs already had a college degree and thus had little interest in or need for a transferable credential or credit. These students were more motivated by gaining additional knowledge and skills, or they were just interested in the MOOC experience for the sake of learning as a goal in and of itself. This squares with the previous history of distance education efforts: as I'll discuss in chapter 2, correspondence courses and radio/television courses (the precursors of MOOCs) attracted mostly older students who often already had a college degree or were often involved in the courses for self-improvement reasons and "edutainment."

While self-improvement, entertainment, or a professional certification of some sort might be of interest to someone who already has a degree or a job, first-year college students are not interested in these things, at least not in the same ways. By definition, these students are at the beginning of their higher education experiences and are still exploring their options. These students want the full experience offered by higher education; they don't want or need single courses for entertainment or self-improvement purposes.

Third, and perhaps most important in terms of sustainability and a business model, the major MOOC providers thought they could attract new college students to their courses based almost entirely on the price of attendance. However, ample evidence suggests that the cost of attendance is not the main reason influencing new college students' decisions about what college to attend. To use a crude analogy: MOOC providers were trying to sell fast food—cheap and mass-produced burgers and fries—to potential diners who were actually interested in the best meal they could afford in a full-service restaurant.

We've long known that the cost of attendance isn't the main reason why first-year colleges students choose universities. The Cooperative Institutional Research Program at the Higher Education Research Institute at UCLA (HERI) has been studying a variety of trends involving new students with "the Freshman Survey" since the early 1970s, polling students on a range of topics including their politics, religion, levels of anxiety about college, and so on, and also why they chose the college they are attending. The report *The American Freshman: National Norms Fall 2016* (Eagan et al. 2017) makes clear there is a growing concern about paying for college. Just over 55 percent of students said they were concerned about paying for college, about 56 percent of first-generation college students said cost was a "very important" factor, and about 58 percent of first-generation students said financial aid offers were "very important" in their decisions about what college to attend. However, the 2016 survey also revealed that the cost of attendance remains in fourth place as to why students made the choice of a particular college, behind "this college has a good academic reputation," "this college's graduates get good jobs," and "this college has a good reputation for its social and extracurricular activities" (Eagan et al. 2017).

I see the results of the HERI surveys playing out in a 10-mile radius of my home. As I've described, the county where I live in southeast Michigan is home to Eastern Michigan University, the University of Michigan, and Washtenaw Community College. EMU is an average regional university, while the University of Michigan is frequently named one of the top twenty-five universities in the world. Most of the students at EMU are from Michigan; most of the students at UM are from out of state. EMU has about 18,000 undergraduate students and about 5,000 graduate students, and UM has about 29,000 undergraduates and about 16,000 graduate students. Washtenaw Community College, which is geographically located between EMU and UM, has about 13,000 students, many of whom are attending part-time and most of whom are from the county. In 2017, tuition at WCC for "in-district" students was just over $2,250 for the year and just over $3,700 for in-state but out-of-district students; at EMU, tuition was just under $10,000 for the year; and at UM, it was just under $15,000 for the year for in-state students (with a slightly higher tuition rate for juniors and seniors), while out-of-state tuition was just shy of $48,000 a year.

Now, if the driving reason for why a student chooses a particular university was costs, then WCC should be the institution in the highest demand, followed by EMU and then UM. In reality, the exact opposite is the case. For all practical purposes, WCC (and most community colleges) admits almost everyone who applies. EMU accepted 68.9 percent of those who applied in 2014, and in 2017, EMU admitted almost 11,000 and enrolled about 2,800 first-year students. The UM's acceptance rate in 2016 was 28.6 percent of those who applied, and in 2017, almost 60,000 students applied (almost 16,000 were admitted and just over 7,000 enrolled). Again, if the cost of attendance was more or as important as the top reason why first-year students choose to attend a particular school, then WCC would be the institution in the county turning students away, UM would be struggling to entice students through its expensive doors, and EMU would presumably be somewhere in the middle, though probably with more selective admission practices. That is not what is happening.

Let me be clear about the issue of the cost of college: tuition and fees in all institutions of higher education in the United States are far too high for all sorts of different reasons, including the systematic de-funding of public education by state governments, the high costs of administration overhead, the labor-intensive nature of institutional education, and out-of-control spending on aspects of the college experience not essential to the educational mission. Football and elaborate student amenities come to mind. The reasons why higher education in the United States is in this financial situation and what we can do about it are complex, but I don't think anyone disagrees with the observable fact that the cost of tuition and fees has been rising too much and too quickly.

Further, as the HERI's reports also show, while the cost of attendance is not the leading reason as to why students choose the schools they choose, it is clear that cost of attendance is more important to new first-year students and their families now than it was a decade ago. The demographics published by HERI are accurate for all new students in the United States, but it is also probably true that there is a level of granularity of these results that differs across different types of institutions. At EMU I've worked with many undergraduates who transferred from WCC after completing a two-year degree, and for many of those students, this approach to earning a bachelor's degree was about saving money.

Nonetheless, students' main reasons for selecting where to attend college still have more to do with the quality of the institution and what it has to offer in terms of programs, reputation, connections, and a social life than with the price of tuition. A free (or very low-cost) MOOC course or degree program that does not have the cultural value of a recognized credential granted by an established higher education institution is not worth the time and effort for would-be students who do not already have a recognized degree. And this, in a nutshell, was why students did not flock to MOOCs: *even for free*, MOOC courses and degrees weren't worth it.

But again, there is obviously much more to the MOOC moment than this abrupt end.

In the next three chapters, I will descend from this high-altitude overview of MOOCs. After describing some of the distance education technologies that were key to the development and rise of MOOCs in the first place, I'll describe and analyze the context within MOOCs themselves from my perspective as a MOOC student and through interviews with MOOC faculty. In the final chapter I will once again return to a broader view of why MOOCs continue to be important, both because of their successes—particularly beyond institutional education—and also as a continuing influencer on trends in online distance education within universities.

## 2

# MOOCS AS A CONTINUATION OF DISTANCE EDUCATION TECHNOLOGIES

In his 2013 TED talk, MIT professor and CEO of the MOOC provider edX, Anant Agarwal begins with an anecdote about the lack of change in classroom space in higher education. "Education hasn't really changed in the past 500 years," he says, showing photos of an MIT lecture hall class from about 50 years ago alongside a contemporary and nearly identical lecture hall class (albeit in color). "The last big innovation in education was the printing press and textbooks. Everything else has changed around us, from healthcare to transportation, everything is different. But education hasn't changed" (Agarwal 2013). Peter Norvig made similar "nothing has changed" claims in his 2012 TED talk. He compared his lecturing technology to the same techniques seen in an illustration from a fourteenth-century manuscript depicting a lecture to university students in Bologna (figure 2.1). "Note the textbook, the sage on the stage, and the sleeping guy in the back, just like today," Norvig (2012) said, and the TED audience chuckled approvingly.

Agarwal and Norvig are obviously employing these opening anecdotes as attention-getting hyperboles, perhaps the key to any memorable TED talk. But unintentionally, they are also examples of one of the most basic misunderstandings that seems to have been widely held by early MOOC enthusiasts, that somehow delivering lecture-based teaching over the internet would be enough to transform higher education as we know it. The examples also ignore all the things that have changed, even in lecture halls. True, teachers and students from 600 or more years ago would recognize the basics of today's lecture hall courses much in the same way we can now visit ancient world ruins and recognize the remains of a theater or a temple. But those students from that fourteenth-century manuscript would likely be amazed by technologies common in lecture halls for some time now—lighting, air conditioning and heating, chalkboards and whiteboards, comfortable seating, let alone video projection, sound

DOI: 10.7330/9781607327875.c002

*Figure. 2.1.* Henricus de Alemannia in Front of His Students *by Laurentius de Voltolina, ca. 1350 (https://commons.wikimedia.org/wiki/File:Laurentius_de_Voltolina_001.jpg)*

systems, and computers. As Alex Reid (2017, 227) has noted, the media environment in face-to-face classrooms—even in lecture halls similar to those that have always existed in universities—now includes digital libraries, social media, laptops, and mobile devices: "Higher education happens online today, regardless of how the courses are catalogued." And, of course, Agarwal, Norvig, and other MOOC entrepreneurs didn't invent online courses either.

This chapter recalls some of the earlier innovations in delivering education in novel and different ways—technologies and pedagogies that fundamentally created the context for the innovation of MOOCs. Specifically, I examine three influential and widespread uses of technology that challenged and changed the traditional notions of a "classroom" experience: correspondence courses, radio and television courses, and what I call, somewhat ironically, "traditional/contemporary" online courses. This is, of course, a woefully incomplete history of distance education in America. For example, I don't discuss the earliest uses of correspondence to teach handwriting, I only briefly touch on the Chautauqua movement and interest in home learning in the nineteenth century, and I don't discuss the important role of the land-grant universities in the United States designated by the Morrill Acts in the nineteenth century and the various extension and outreach programs still sponsored by these institutions. Each of these moments represents another example of the historical context that led to the MOOC phenomenon. I focus here on correspondence, radio/television, and contemporary online courses because each of these technologies has clearly traceable analogies and connections to MOOCs as we know them now:

- Each of these distance education technologies was developed both as a sincere effort to extend opportunity to would-be students who were otherwise disenfranchised from higher education and, simultaneously, as a means for both nonprofit educational institutions and for-profit education entrepreneurs to make money.
- After a time of trendiness, when these innovations were seen by some as a "threat" to traditional higher education, each faded into the background, either remaining in the mix as an alternative for delivering higher education or absorbed into media and learning opportunities beyond the university.
- Each of these innovations in distance education begs the fundamental question that continues to be asked with MOOCs and their progeny: What exactly *is* an "education" and what (and who) is it for?

## CORRESPONDENCE

In the middle of my final term as an undergraduate at the University of Iowa in 1988, while I was busy making plans for the MFA program in fiction writing I would be starting in just a few months at Virginia Commonwealth University in Richmond—a new apartment, new friends, the exciting and unnerving prospect of teaching for the first time as a graduate assistant—I discovered I was four credits short of graduation as a result of testing out of the Gen Ed writing and speech course at the beginning of my freshman year. Testing out meant the course requirement had been waived, which was not the same thing as receiving credit, thus the shortfall. Because it was the middle of the term, simply adding a couple more normal courses was not possible, and summer school was far from an ideal option. I had to finish my undergraduate degree before I could begin my graduate studies. Things were looking grim.

Fortunately, a now long-forgotten academic adviser helped me think quickly. At the time, Iowa's physical education classes ran for half a semester, and I believe the one-credit course I enrolled in was called "Relaxation," which was about just that. For forty-five minutes two or three times a week, my fellow students and I met in a room with a padded floor learning various relaxation techniques. Successful students fell asleep. I still use some of the things I learned in that class, actually.

Since there were no available options for any other three-credit courses, this adviser suggested a correspondence course. According to the 1986–1988 General Catalog for the University of Iowa, the Division of Continuing Education offered 160 "Guided Correspondence Study courses" offered by forty-two different departments. With my adviser's help, I enrolled in a creative writing course. I received a packet in the mail from the instructor with various exercises and readings, but instead of working through those materials, I wrote a letter explaining my situation and sent the teacher the same portfolio of short stories that had helped me gain admittance to the MFA program. As I recall, after I corresponded with the teacher back and forth a bit, I passed the class (I believe I earned an A), and my delayed graduation crisis was averted.

I tell this story for two reasons. First, while my focus here is on the *origins* of correspondence courses at the turn of the nineteenth and twentieth centuries, courses delivered by postal mail are still a part of the accepted curriculum at major universities in this country (though most of these correspondence courses have morphed into online offerings). Second, while I do believe that my own experiences in a correspondence course were not typical in that I was more or less demonstrating what I had already learned rather than having learned something new, I have to say that my ability to get credit for a course where I didn't so much "learn" as submitted work on what I had previously accomplished now gives me pause.

Correspondence study in America emerged in the nineteenth century as both a response and a complement to earlier nontraditional learning environments. Home study, women's clubs predicated on study (particularly before women were admitted to public colleges), and literary study groups were remarkably popular in that century, both as a form of social engagement and "entertainment" but also as viable alternatives to higher education, which itself was much less defined than we think of it today. As Joseph F. Kett (1994, 149) notes, "Prior to the 1890s 'higher education' had loose connotations. Not only were degree-granting colleges abundant, but the distinction between them and the vast number of academies, 'seminaries,' 'collegiate institutions,' and high schools was far from clear." In fact, as Labaree (2017, 28) notes in his discussion of the rise of higher education in the United States in this era, "For students, it was often a choice of going to high school or to college rather than seeing one as the feeder institution for the other . . .

And some high schools offered a program of studies that was superior to the offerings at many colleges."

One of the most influential of these "loosely connected" educational phenomena in this era was the Chautauqua Institution and Movement. The institution was a place: it was founded in 1874 in Chautauqua, New York, on a site near Chautauqua Lake by Methodist ministers Lewis Miller and John Heyl Vincent. While it began as a Bible study experience and was (and remains) rooted in Christian values and teachings, the institution quickly evolved into a program of courses covering the arts, music, theater, writing, languages, and other liberal arts. In 1878 the institution expanded its offerings in the form of correspondence study, offered both as an educational experience similar to what was available from the colleges and schools of the time and also as an alternative to the less virtuous vices of the time: "The four-year, correspondence course was one of the first attempts at distance learning. Besides broadening access to education, the CLSC [Chautauqua Literary and Scientific Circle] program was intended to show people how best to use their leisure time and avoid the growing availability of idle pastimes, such as drinking, gambling, dancing and theater-going, that posed a threat both to good morals and to good health. To share the cost of purchasing the publications and to take encouragement from others in the course, students were encouraged to form local CLSC reading circles" ("Our History" n.d.).

The correspondence courses and reading circles eventually led to the movement, which included other independent and permanently located Chautauqua sites (known as "Daughter Chautauquas") all over the United States, particularly in rural communities in the Midwest and West, and also "circuit" or "tent" Chautauquas, which were traveling shows that featured speakers and performers—again, as an alternative to the "idle pastimes" made possible with increased leisure time in late nineteenth-century/ early twentieth-century America. Circuit Chautauquas persisted into the early twentieth century, attracting as many as 30 million Americans annually as late as 1924. Incidentally, Chautauquas are not a completely forgotten phenomenon. Several "Daughter Chautauquas" still exist and conduct annual programs, and the original Chautauqua Institution in New York offers a full nine-week program of summer courses, lectures, and performances attended by more than 100,000 annually; in addition, more than 8,000 "students enroll annually in the Chautauqua Summer Schools" ("Our History" n.d.). Today's Chautauqua Institution also offers a variety of more modern amenities and recreational activities—including golf, sailing, tennis, and a fitness center.

According to Barbara L. Watkins, this was "a quite radical idea: the invention and elaboration of collegiate correspondence study," and support for the Chautauqua movement generally and the correspondence courses specifically came from a number of prominent university faculty of their day. The most famous was William Rainey Harper who was a child prodigy, having graduated from college at fourteen and finished his postgraduate studies at Yale in 1876 at the age of twenty. He directed the Chautauqua College of Liberal Arts from 1883 to 1891, which "was authorized by the state of New York to grant academic degrees to students who successfully completed work at the summer institutes and by correspondence during the year" (Watkins 1991, 4). In 1890, John D. Rockefeller asked Harper to organize and become the first president of the University of Chicago, which, in the 1892–1893 school year, opened and enrolled both conventional and correspondence students. In Watkins's (1991, 4) view, while the Chautauqua movement "helped pave the way for university extension" and correspondence courses, it also resulted in the decline in popularity of Chautauqua's educational mission, since programs like the Chautauqua College of Liberal Arts were taken over by better funded and already established universities.

Among his many other accomplishments, Harper is also remembered for his charming prediction about the future place of correspondence study in higher education: "The day is coming when the work done by correspondence will be greater in amount than that done in the classrooms of our academies and colleges; when the students who shall recite by correspondence will far outnumber those who make oral recitations" (Noble 2001, 10). I first encountered this passage from Harper in David F. Noble's *Digital Diploma Mills*, a scathing critique of online teaching, which I'll return to later in this chapter. In Noble's book, Harper comes across as humorously at odds with history, in the same league as those who predicted that the telephone would never catch on, that airplanes were impossible, and that television was a passing fad. The reality of Harper's words is more complicated, however.

Harper's prediction is part of a long section he contributed to John Heyl Vincent's *The Chautauqua Movement*, a book published in 1886 that is part personal narrative, part history of the movement he helped define, and also a vision of what can best be described as Vincent's hopes for what the Chautauqua movement might become. Harper's contribution appears in chapter 8, "The College of Liberal Arts," in a section titled "The 'Correspondence' System Defined and Defended by Dr. Harper"; it's the only section of the book not written by Vincent, which makes it all the more strange a contribution. It's worth spending a moment with this section by Harper because, in addition to clarifying what he actually meant by his prediction about the future of correspondence study, it spells out Harper's appraisal of the disadvantages and advantages of correspondence courses in language that is clearly applicable to contemporary distance education.

He begins by outlining the basic process of the assignments and coursework and then offers this critical qualification: "From this it [can] be seen that the correspondence-teacher must be pains-taking, patient, sympathetic, and *alive*; and that the correspondence-pupil must be earnest, ambitious, appreciative, and likewise *alive*. Whatever a *dead* teacher may accomplish in the classroom, he can do nothing by correspondence; and if a student lacking the qualities just named undertake[s] work by correspondence, one of two things will happen: either he will acquire these qualities, and succeed; or he will remain as he was at the beginning, and fail. The man who does the work at all must do it well" (Vincent 1886, 185, original emphasis).

Harper's insistence on the *aliveness* and hard work of both teachers and students continues, first in his explanation of the disadvantages of correspondence study. Harper's vision of the problems of correspondence study is similar to the objections that persist with distance education. Correspondence students lack the personal connection to an instructor and to other students present in "the recitation-room" (Vincent 1886, 185), and traditional teaching includes a lot of material not included or easily relatable in textbooks and similar materials. Correspondence students spend less time on their studies than face-to-face students, and they do so with more irregularity and interruptions. Correspondence students have to write out all of their work, which "is in sharp contrast with the freedom and pleasure with which others make an oral recitation" (Vincent 1886, 186). Correspondence students are also more likely to cheat and to not finish the course because, in Harper's view, the courses are more difficult: "Whatever the common opinion may be, the requirements of the correspondence-system are of so exacting and rigid a nature as to prevent some from completing the work, who would certainly be able to pass through the course of study in many of our so-called colleges" (Vincent 1886, 187).

Harper addresses each of these disadvantages in the order he presented them. He argues that the "personal stimulus furnished by the teacher" might be useful for many students but perhaps valueless two-thirds of the time, "for it is safe to assert that two out of three teachers exert no such influence upon their pupils, their work being purely mechanical" (Vincent 1886, 187). Harper says the "class-spirit" is not completely lacking in correspondence courses, and it might even be "inspiring" for correspondence students to realize they were in a shared class with other students who were all over the country "and even in foreign lands" (Vincent 1886, 187). While correspondence study lacks the quantity of face-to-face "recitations," it makes up for it in the quality because the work has to be completed in writing. The interruptions faced by correspondence students are "mitigated by the fact that the average correspondence-student is thirty years of age, and therefore old enough to overcome the bad effect of such interruptions" (Vincent 1886, 188); unlike the situation in face-to-face courses, when students miss class for some reason, correspondence students can easily make up the work at a different time.

But while clearly a supporter of correspondence study, Harper did not mean it as a replacement for traditional college classrooms (or "oral instruction"):

> These are some of the advantages of the correspondence-system. But is any one to suppose that there exists, in the mind of those especially interested in this system, a desire to have it take the place of oral instruction? Is the one in any sense a rival of the other? I wish here to record, in answer to these questions, a most emphatic No. What is the fact? Only those persons are encouraged to study by correspondence, or, indeed, admitted to such study, who because of age, poverty, occupation, situation or some other good reason, cannot avail themselves of oral instruction. Away, therefore, with all baseless and foolish prejudice in this matter! The correspondence system would not, if it could, supplant oral instruction, or be regarded as its substitute. There is a field for each which the other cannot fill. Let each to its proper work. (Vincent 1886, 191–192)

What Harper *really* seems to have meant in his comment "the work done by correspondence will be greater in amount than that done in the classrooms of our academies" is that extending correspondence education to the masses through the Chautauqua College of Liberal Arts study meant there would be more students in that program than in traditional universities. Correspondence study was not a replacement for traditional college; rather, Harper imagined just the opposite: "By enlisting sixty or seventy thousand people (many of whom are parents) in a course of English reading which embraces the subjects of the college course, [correspondence study] makes them familiar with the college world, and thus prepares them to insist that their own children shall enter that world as college students" (Vincent 1886, 193).

In the 1880s the average college or university in the United States had 123 students, and only twenty-six institutions in the country had more than 200 students (Labaree 2017, 41). But by the late 1920s and early 1930s, there was a "newfound utility of going to college" in the United States, particularly to prepare for particular occupations and professions (Labaree 2017, 74), and enrollments soared.

As conventional college enrollments increased, Harper's prediction of the day when correspondence students would outnumber those in classrooms also came to pass, though those correspondence and home study students were probably not the college students Harper had in mind. The most widely cited book of the period about correspondence study, Walton Simon Bittner and Mervey Foster Mallory's 1933 *University Teaching by Mail*, lists about forty universities as members of the National University Extension Association offering correspondence courses. Most were state universities, and several offered courses either exclusively or predominantly for non-credit. Correspondence courses in private and proprietary schools grew at a dramatically faster rate. According to Bittner and Mallory (1933), there were about 200,000 "active enrollments" of students in correspondence courses sponsored by traditional public institutions.

In the same time period, there were somewhere between 1.5 million and 2 million students enrolled in proprietary correspondence schools. The subjects students in proprietary schools studied were a far cry from Harper's courses in Hebrew and Latin. According to Kett, "Correspondence schools offered instruction in an astonishing range of topics," everything from farming, missionary and Bible work, osteopathy, and embalming to less exotic and more business-oriented courses like bookkeeping and stenography to courses in a whole host of trades. The correspondence courses offered by universities often granted high school or college credit; proprietary correspondence schools did not, "despite their occasional claims to the contrary" (Kett 1994, 236). The most famous of the proprietary correspondence schools in the early twentieth century was the International Correspondence Schools (ICS) of Scranton, Pennsylvania. In the early days, ICS's students were coal miners hoping to qualify as mine inspectors and foremen: "Few possessed the knowledge of arithmetical fractions necessary to calculate the flow of air through mine passages, or the ability to identify the different gases in mines. With families to support, most were too busy or too embarrassed by their ignorance to attend night schools" (Kett 1994, 236–237).

The critiques and roles of proprietary schools of the early twentieth century were not significantly different than those of the proprietary schools today. "Although occasionally prone to fraud and always characterized by brazen advertising, correspondence schools pioneered innovative educational methods and forged close and mutually beneficial ties to major corporations" (Kett 1994, 236), though that partnership between the worlds of education and corporations was controversial then and continues to be controversial now. For example, the ICS soon increased its reach and enrollments by developing more courses, advertising extensively, and, as early as 1906, employing salesmen "to canvass 'prospects' and to engage in 'inspirational' advertising and solicitation" (Kett 1994, 237).

In contrast, most of the correspondence courses offered through traditional universities mirrored the bricks and mortar curriculum: courses in English composition, literature, algebra, history, education, and so on. The specifics about how these courses were offered and for what type of credit varied, but I'd like to dwell for a moment on one specific and local example. For a different research project years ago, I read a 1938 University of Michigan MA thesis by Anthony Matulis (1938) titled "A Study of the Supervised College Correspondence Study Department as Sponsored by the Extension Division of the University of Michigan." As the title suggests, Matulis's thesis was about the correspondence study program at the University of Michigan in the mid-1930s. This wasn't a for-profit enterprise, at least not when Matulis was doing his research; rather, it was a Depression-era welfare program sponsored by the federal government through the Works Progress Administration and the state of Michigan through the Emergency Education Program. These assistance programs paid for mailing costs, tuition for students, and pay for instructors. Both students and teachers needed to demonstrate dramatic financial hardship to qualify for this program. The UM program also had a bit of a hybrid approach in that it ran various study centers around the state staffed by graduate students and part-time instructors. It's not clear how many of these correspondence students eventually went on to earn degrees, but as Harper and others before him argued, Matulis (1938, 65) points out the benefit of reaching students who otherwise would have no such access to higher education: "No statistical tables could be formed to show the mental satisfaction received by tired housewives to whom the study of the vastness of history opened new doors, by shut-ins who reached beyond their beds through facile pens, or by factory workers who had new vistas stretched before them by means of their readings in sociology or political science."

Interestingly, the demographics across all correspondence courses were similar in that they were the same kinds of nontraditional students who have now found their way into MOOCs—this despite the fact that MOOC providers were initially assuming an audience similar to traditional college students. Most of the students in proprietary correspondence schools were not college-bound and interested in training for certification or what we might today call "just in time" education. But students enrolled in correspondence courses through traditional universities were also different demographically from students attending universities at the time. Bittner and Mallory (1933, 32–33) say that students were "of every age and occupation, male and female, married and unmarried, successful and unsuccessful, respectable people, and persons in prison" and that university correspondence (rather than proprietary correspondence) courses "appeal chiefly to the 'educated,' to those who seek to complete and round out formal schooling, and to those also who are interested in study for its own sake." Most universities reported significantly more women than men enrolled, and, also not unlike contemporary MOOCs, correspondence students were older and frequently already held college degrees.

In 1930, Abraham Flexner wrote an influential critique of higher education, *Universities: American, English, German*, which was an expansion on lectures Flexner gave at Oxford in 1928. Flexner was a well-known intellectual and educator, notably for the *Flexner Report*. That book-length study, published in 1910 on behalf of the Carnegie Foundation, was a critique of medical education in the United States and Canada, and it reshaped American medical schools in terms of admission and graduation requirements in ways that are still evident today. Flexner also served as the "general secretary of the Rockefeller-funded General Education Board and later became the founding director of the Institute for Advanced Study at Princeton" (Noble 2001, 16).

Overall, Flexner's complaint against higher education was that it was too cozy with the corporate world. His complaints are voluminous, purple-prosed, and, in a curious way, remarkably current in terms of the common criticisms leveled against higher education today. For example, this critique of college sports is still relevant on my campus: "There is not a college or university in America that has the courage to place athletics where every one perfectly well knows they belong. On the contrary . . . proportionately more money is spent on college athletics than on any legitimate college activity. The football coach is better known to the student body and the general public than the president; the professors are, on the average, less highly remunerated" (Flexner 1930, 65).

And consider this passage, which could just as easily be a complaint today about the ways universities supposedly coddle students with their amenities and "trigger warnings":

Every jerk and shock must be eliminated; the students must be "oriented"; they must be "advised" as to what to "take"; they must be vocationally guided. How is it possible to educate persons who will never be permitted to burn their fingers, who must be dexterously and expensively housed, first as freshmen, then as upperclassmen, so as to make the right sort of social connections and to establish the right sort of social relationships, who are protected against risk as they should be protected against plague, and who, even though "they work their way through," have no conception of the effort required to develop intellectual sinew? (Flexner 1930, 68)

In terms of correspondence and home study programs specifically, Flexner is particularly critical of the University of Chicago and Columbia University (then Columbia College), both of which offered and advertised extensive correspondence programs—many of which seemed to blur the distinction between the courses offered by traditional universities and for-profit proprietary schools. Most of the for-credit correspondence courses seemed to be targeted to help students earn a high school (rather than a bachelor's) degree, and while both schools offered "serious subjects in a serious fashion" through correspondence, Flexner was appalled at the range of courses in fields like "principles of advertising," "practical poultry raising," "newspaper practice," "business writing," and "wrestling, judo, and self-defense," just to mention a few of the course titles Flexner highlights. The problem with these courses is that they simply are not within the mission of a university:

> Columbia College is not a vocational school; vocational training may be ever so important, but the confusion of all sorts of training—vocational, domestic, scientific, cultural, in high school and college—harms all alike and harms the highest most of all. It is defended on the ground already mentioned that America is a democratic country, which, for large social reasons, ignores distinctions. But America does not ignore all distinctions. It simply ignores the real distinctions; and not all the weight of its wealth and number can place cooking and wrestling and typewriting on an intellectual par with music, science, literature, and economics, or make it sound educational procedure to jumble them together. (Flexner 1930, 56)

In other words, Flexner's (1930, 147) main complaint is about the "vocational" content of too many correspondence courses rather than the method of instruction per se: "Now, correspondence courses may have their uses; and in a country where postage is cheap and superficiality rampant, they are likely to spring up." Vocational training in the form of correspondence courses, home study, and extension programs did not belong in anything called a university—though he hardly stopped there. Labaree (2017, 59) argues that Flexner thought "the only thing that made an institution 'university grade' was the graduate school in pure form—where professors performed research and where they edu-cated advanced graduate students who planned to become researchers themselves or members of high professions." Flexner (according to Labaree) saw little difference between undergraduate programs and high school, and he thought this education "should be carried out elsewhere in order to avoid polluting the graduate enterprise." While professional schools in medicine and law were acceptable in Flexner's vision of the university, schools of education, business, or anything else that suggested the vocational belonged elsewhere (Labaree 2017, 59).

Bittner and Mallory's *University Teaching by Mail* was written in part as a response to Flexner's *Universities*, and they occasionally respond to him directly: "Mr. Flexner, for instance, has an attitude that seems to reflect that of other less articulate critics of the American university who suspect any of the service functions that have been added to the old university of scholarly research and academic lecturing" (Bittner and Mallory 1933, 2). They go on:

> Schools of education, of commerce, of journalism, of domestic arts, and divisions of extension and adult education appear to one type of critic as hardly liberal, scholarly, or properly selective. Such an attitude is stub-bornly maintained and will probably not yield to any argument but may yield to the necessity of dealing with certain facts. And the facts show undoubtedly that the modern university of America, in many a notable case, is, whether we like it or not, more and more a public service institu-tion. It does undoubtedly perform functions that are utilitarian as well as cultural. And who shall say that the useful may not be cultural? It does conduct courses of instruction for diverse groups, for varied types of indi-viduals on many levels of preparation, who are not selected for intellectual scholarship alone. (Bittner and Mallory 1933, 3)

Thus the controversy over correspondence study—again, like the controversy over other innovations in distance education delivery, including MOOCs—is at least as much about the definition of higher education as it is about technology. Flexner (1930, 2) believed the university should strive to maintain its intellectual mission and change slowly: "Universities must at times give society, not what society wants, but what it needs." Bittner and Mallory (1933, 5) dismiss the value of maintaining "the more ancient type of cloistered college and university" in the face of modern progress, for "aloofness has its dangers."

In a pattern we'll see repeated in radio and television courses and also with traditional online courses, correspondence courses had their rise and their fall, but they did not entirely fade away. As I mentioned in the opening of this section, correspondence courses continue to be offered by both traditional universities and proprietary institutions today. The enormous International Correspondence Schools of Scranton remained open throughout the twentieth century and "transitioned" into the proprietary and online Penn Foster, which continues to offer both high school and college courses and is still headquartered in Scranton. And, as Labaree (2017, 60) argues, the inclusion of robust undergraduate programs, vocational courses, and professional schools Flexner so strongly objected to led to a "golden age" of higher education.

### RADIO, TELEVISION, AND *SESAME STREET*

Experiments in the use of radio and television in distance education are as old as the mediums themselves, though, unlike correspondence courses, they were generally seen as a supplement to traditional higher education offerings rather than a replacement. Interestingly, while radio and television obviously helped define popular culture in the twentieth century, neither proved to be successful means for delivering institutional education. Instead, both eventually became the non-commercial public broadcasting venues that are still with us, channels and stations that broadcast news, cultural, and educational (arguably, even MOOC-like) content.

Radio didn't fail as an educational medium out of a lack of effort. Carroll Atkinson's *Radio Extension Courses Broadcast for Credit*, published in 1941, is a catalog and summary of dozens of different initiatives, including the previously mentioned program at the University of Michigan that was sponsored in part through the Works Progress Administration in the 1930s. The university didn't have a radio station of its own at the time but made arrangements with a "large station" in Detroit. According to Fred G. Stevenson, the person in charge of distance education at Michigan (and quoted extensively by Atkinson [1941, 39]), "All correspondence students were notified in advance of the time of these broadcasts. The talks were more largely inspirational and informative than directly concerned with instruction in the course—the latter being handled entirely by correspondence." That said, the programming was particularly important for foreign language classes where "we thought it was necessary for the student to hear the actual language which they were studying" (Atkinson 1941, 39). Because of the limited access, the radio portion of these correspondence courses ended after only two years. Stevenson, perhaps anticipating the future use of technologies to facilitate hybrid learning, lamented the loss of the radio component, saying "in my judgement a good combination should be worked out between radio and correspondence instruction" (cited in Atkinson 1941, 39).

This short-lived experiment at Michigan was typical of the promises and failures of radio, and Atkinson's bitterness about this failure in the opening pages of his book is palpable. He was convinced that radio was a means of extending "to the masses [educational services] in harmony with the American democratic ideals of equal opportunities for all who seek them"; the problem was educators unwilling to change what they were doing: "So long as professional educators continue to maintain a holier-than-thou conception that they possess exclusively the secret patented formula on how to improve the intellectual welfare of the human race without recognizing the necessity of changing from time-honored methods of the past to meet the highly increased tempo of modern times, just that long will they fail to see and utilize the true educational possibilities of radio communication" (Atkinson 1941, 12).

Arguably, television enjoyed more success than radio, particularly in the 1960s and 1970s. Probably the most famous example of these projects was *Sunrise Semester*, which was a cooperation between New York University and CBS television between 1957 and 1982 to broadcast college lectures early in the morning. As Deborah Shapiro (2015) recalled in the NYU alumni web publication *Connect*, "The program allowed qualified viewers to receive academic credit for watching. There were curricula, reading lists, and mail-in assignments and exams. In lieu of office hours, registered students could write in questions to their instructors, who were NYU professors recruited by the Office of Radio-Television." The first course was "Comparative Literature 10: From Stendhal to Hemingway," and Shapiro (2015) describes the course as "a hit": "The entertainment magazine *Variety* called it 'the first unquestioned hit show of the 1957 television season.' Though only 177 students were enrolled, Dr. Zulli had 74,000 viewers in his first week; by the end of the semester, 120,000 New Yorkers were waking up to watch the 6:30 telecast. They weren't just watching, either: New York City bookstores sold out of the course's required reading so rapidly that Random House needed to issue a reprint of Stendhal's *The Red and the Black*."

One of those enrolled and paying students, Mrs. Cora Gay Carr, was the subject of a 1962 *New York Times* feature article. While she initially registered for the courses "just for intellectual kicks," she went on to earn fifty-four credits from television courses, and Carr credits the program with motivating her to return to college as a full-time student. And, in a passage that describes both the main demographic for *Sunrise Semester* and also the social norms of the times, Carr reports that her husband, a lawyer, approved: "He thinks it's fine because I'm up so early and can finish so much of the homework in good time" (Shepard 1962, L 55).

*Sunrise Semester* was far from the only television for-credit program, and Leslie N. Purdy recalls many of the successes of both mediums. There were experiments in using television for educational purposes as early as 1933, and "by the 1940s, elementary and secondary schools were beginning to experiment with programs offered by commercial television stations" (Purdy 1980, 17). The Chicago TV College was a particularly successful and important experiment in educational television. The program began in 1956, and, summarizing Jame Zigerell and Hymen Chausow's 1974 *Chicago's TV College: A Fifth Report*, more than 80,000 students officially enrolled for credit through City Colleges of Chicago; about 2,200 students graduating with an AA degree took on average one semester of coursework via television; and "about 400 students [were] awarded an AA degree for study entirely by television" (Purdy 1980, 19). In fact, City Colleges of Chicago offered courses that involved some "teleweb" elements that only ended in 2015.

But, like radio, enthusiasm for the television experiment ultimately faded, and for similar reasons. For universities and programs that relied on commercial broadcast for support, offering courses through the radio and television was not economically sustainable, and these experiments were well before the "hundreds of channels" landscape of cable. An episode of *Sunrise Semester* running at 6:30 a.m. was only practical while there was no commercial interest in the time slot; once commercial interest arrived, the show was pushed out. Programs like *Chicago TV College* lasted as long as they did because of the connection with educational and now public television—in this case, the Chicago station WTTW.

One of the other shortcomings of educational television was a "lack of courseware" and course productions that took advantage of television's "unique characteristics as a medium" (Purdy 1980, 21). Not unlike the first wave of MOOCs (as I will discuss in chapter 3), the preferred mode of production for educational television in this era was to simply put the instructor in front of the camera and record the lecture. Purdy (1980, 21) quotes from Judith Murphy and Ronald Gross's lament in their 1966 *Learning by Television*, suggesting that little had changed between their study and Purdy's 1980 article (and, arguably, since Harper's 1885 critique of "dead" teaching): "Few educators have used the new technology to help bring about a basic change in instruction, and there has been little relating of television to other new media and technologies. As a matter of fact, the most conspicuous result of television teaching has been an incidental byproduct: the medium has displayed in public what had heretofore gone on behind many closed classroom doors—uninspired teaching."

But these experiments in educational radio and television didn't end entirely; rather, they were a part of the development of the "public" broadcast system we have today. The Corporation for Public Broadcasting was created in 1967 as part of that year's Public Broadcasting Act, and the creation of the Public Broadcasting System (PBS) and National Public Radio (NPR) and the wide variety of educational/"edutainment" programming available all belong to that system.

This brings me to *Sesame Street*.

In June 2015, economists Melissa S. Kearney of the University of Maryland and Phillip B. Levine of Wellesley College published a working paper, "Early Childhood Education by MOOC: Lessons from *Sesame Street*," that was part of a National Bureau of Economic Research project. As they explain in the abstract, Kearney and Levine were building on previous research that provided evidence that "watching the show generated an immediate and sizable increase in test scores" by researching more specifically the variables of how the show was broadcast via VHF and UHF stations. Their results indicated that "preschool-aged children in areas with better reception when it was introduced were more likely to advance through school as appropriate for their age" (Kearney and Levine abstract, n.p.) Interestingly, other than a few footnotes, only one paragraph near the beginning of the thirty-nine-page paper mentions MOOCs:

> An analysis of the effectiveness of *Sesame Street* can potentially also inform current discussions regarding the ability of Massive Open Online Courses (MOOCs) to deliver educational improvements. In essence, *Sesame Street* was the first MOOC. Although MOOCs differ in what they entail, *Sesame Street* satisfies the basic feature of electronic transmission of online educational material. Both *Sesame Street* and MOOCs provide educational interventions at a fraction of the cost of more traditional classroom settings. Most (but not all) MOOCs exist at the level of higher education, which clearly differs from a preschool intervention. Our knowledge of the ability of MOOCs to improve outcomes for its participants is so limited, though, that any proper evaluation of the impact of electronic transmission of educational content is beneficial. (Kearney and Levine 2015a, 2)

Kearney and Levine's essay continues with an analysis of test scores, demographic data, and television broadcasting data to correlate their argument in economic terms. Frankly, I will have to take Kearney and Levine's word for it regarding the validity of the main claims of their paper—that children who lived in areas with better reception for *Sesame Street* benefited with subsequently higher test scores—since its economic methodologies are beyond my area of expertise. However, I am comfortable asserting that Kearney and Levine's essay has nothing to do with MOOCs.

If Kearney and Levine's goal in their title and passing reference to MOOCs was to shine some mainstream media attention on their study, it worked. Articles about the study ran in *Business Insider*, the *Atlantic*, the *Washington Post*, and many other magazines and newspapers. Not surprisingly, Kearney and Levine faced stiff criticism from MOOC researchers. Rolin Moe (2015) put it succinctly: "Using MOOC in the title of their paper provided an avenue for hype and clickbait." Audrey Watters (2015) piled on, arguing that "*Sesame Street* was not the first MOOC. And really, it is not a MOOC at all. To argue such—to offer that analogy—is historically flawed, erasing other earlier educational media." Watters goes on in some detail to describe some of that history and also to dive further into Kearney and Levine's methodologies and claims. Even Kearney and Levine (2015b) had to tamp down some of the ways their article was "spun" in the mainstream media, writing on the *New Republic* website that they do not mean to suggest that *Sesame Street* was a substitute for other, more traditional interventions: "We should not swap one good thing for another. Rather, we support the role that TV and technology more generally can play in assisting parents, caregivers, teachers, and policymakers to augment more traditional preschool interventions. This is most important not for the kids whose parents are using TV as an occasional break from more intensive forms of enrichment, but rather for the kids who do not have the benefit of enriching and educational activities all day long." They did repeat the claim, though, that *Sesame Street* was "essentially the first MOOC, providing educational content to millions of viewers for free."

Watters, Moe, and others are clearly correct in pointing out that *Sesame Street* was not a MOOC, if for no other reason than it doesn't share any of the key features that define MOOCs—it lacks direct interactivity, it is not delivered via the internet, it isn't at all a "course," it's not possible to take it for credit, and so on. Further, to the extent that any television show qualified as having the qualities of a massive open online course, it seems to me that the real "first MOOCs" were the actual for-credit courses offered through *Sunrise Semester, Chicago TV College,* and similar programs in the 1950s, 1960s, and 1970s. If anything, *Sesame Street* derived from these programs and not the other way around.

Still, I find this blip in the news about *Sesame Street* as an early example of a MOOC thought-provoking. One of the goals of *Sesame Street* when it first premiered in the late 1960s was to reach students (in this case, pre-schoolers) who were otherwise disenfranchised from access to education. At the same time and also like MOOCs, there has always been a financial motive behind *Sesame Street,* first in terms of sustainability, and now, with the program's new arrangement with HBO (not to mention the profits from *Sesame Street*—themed toys, books, movies, and other spin-offs), the producers of the show seem to be chasing profits. *Sesame Street* has gone from being a leader in educational television for children to being one of many: that is, it has become an accepted part of the kind of educational television we have come to expect to be available through outlets like PBS and the many cable networks targeted to children. And again, the research many others have done regarding the impact of *Sesame Street* on children (including Kearney and Levine's research) highlights the ongoing questions being raised by the MOOC moment and beyond: What constitutes learning versus institutional education, where does it happen, how do we measure it, and what is it for?

## TRADITIONAL/CONTEMPORARY ONLINE EDUCATION

In discussing both correspondence study and what I am calling "traditional/contemporary" online education, I am indebted to David F. Noble and his 2001 book *Digital Diploma Mills*. In fact, the first chapter of Noble's book is titled "Lessons from a Pre-Digital Age: The Correspondence Education Movement," and it covers much of the same territory I discussed earlier in this chapter. Sadly, Noble died suddenly in 2010. While he did not publish any writings specifically about MOOCs, it is easy to extrapolate his position on them from *Digital Diploma Mills*. I'm also reliant here on my own personal history because while I have never been a student in a traditional/contemporary online course, I've been teaching online since 2005.

Experiments in offering courses in part or entirely online date back to the 1980s and before, when access to what we know now as the internet was accomplished with phone modems that transmit data seventy times slower than the wifi network in a typical coffee shop. The first online courses for undergraduate and graduate credit began in 1986, the first "large-scale online course" was offered through the United Kingdom's Open University in 1989, and the proprietary school the University of Phoenix began its online programs in 1989 as well.

The rise of traditional/contemporary online courses parallels the growth of the internet, particularly with the invention of the World Wide Web and graphic user interface web browsers in the early 1990s. Michael Moore and Greg Kearsley (2005, 43) report that in 1995, only 9 percent of American adults accessed the internet. By 2002, 66 percent of Americans were online, and over 80 percent of public universities offered courses online. The increasing popularity of online courses in traditional universities parallels the development of the even more rapid rise of online courses and degrees at proprietary institutions, notably the University of Phoenix. In 2003, Phoenix had more than 70,000 students and 4,000 online instructors, and almost all of those instructors taught part-time (Moore and Kearsley 2005, 60).

Noble (2001) argues that this rise of traditional/contemporary online courses through the likes of the University of Phoenix is an existential threat to higher education, particularly as major universities abandon the higher values of their educational missions and become cozier with corporate interests. In other words, in his critique of traditional/ contemporary online courses, Noble is channeling Abraham Flexner's complaints about correspondence courses.

Like Flexner, Noble (2001) draws a distinction between "education" and what belongs in a university and vocational "training." Noble (2001, 2) admits that training is "arguably more suitable for distance delivery," though that doesn't make training something that is at all empowering: "In essence, training involves the honing of a person's mind so that his or her mind can be used for the purposes of someone other than that person. Training thus typically entails a radical divorce between knowledge and the self." He goes on to define education as "the exact opposite of training in that it entails not the dissociation but the utter integration of knowledge and the self, in a word, self-knowledge." Education—again, in contrast to "training"—is about relationships between students and teachers, about collective self-knowledge, and it is a "process of becoming for all parties, based upon mutual recognition and validation and catering upon the formation and evolution of identity" (Noble 2001, 2). Noble (2001, 3) goes on to critique the familiar apparatus of higher education—"syllabi, lectures, lessons, exams (now referred to in the aggregate as 'content')"—as more examples of the commodification of education, where the "educational experience" is distilled into "discrete, reified, and ultimately salable things or packages of things."

For Noble, the introduction of traditional/contemporary online courses is a repetition of the problems of the correspondence education movement a century before. Again, like Flexner, he saw nothing but despair in the relationship among higher education, vocational training, and commercial enterprises: "For-profit commercial firms are once again emerging to provide vocational training to working people via computer-based distance instruction. Universities are once again striving to meet the challenge of these commercial enterprises, generate new revenue streams, and extend the range and reach of their offerings. And although trying somehow to distinguish themselves from their commercial rivals—while collaborating ever more closely with them—they are once again coming to resemble them, this time as digital diploma mills" (Noble 2001, 5).

After the opening chapter in which he describes the rise and fall of correspondence schools (more or less from Flexner's point of view), Noble spends most of *Digital Diploma Mills* sounding the alarm about the rise of traditional/contemporary online courses and the problematic relationship between corporate interests in universities. For example, in describing the creation of Western Governors University in the mid-1990s, Noble (2001, 30) argues that WGU was "the most ambitious US effort to date" for the commercialization and market orientation of higher education. He points out that start-up funds for WGU "come from the private sector, specifically from Education Management Group, the educational arm of the world's largest educational publisher, Simon and Schuster" (Noble 2001, 31), and notes that then Utah governor and WGU co-chair Michael Levitt once claimed that "in the future an institution of higher education will become a little like a local television station" (Noble 2001, 59)—meaning that the purpose of most universities would simply be to "rebroadcast" existing and branded content. WGU is just one of the partnerships Noble analyzes and critiques; others include corporate education enterprises such as Onlinelearning.net, the Home Education Network (THEN) (www.then.com), a start-up company partnered with the University of Chicago called UNNEXT.com, and others.

Obviously, the proponents of these partnerships saw these initiatives in ways similar to those who favored correspondence and television courses: the goal was to extend learning to those who are otherwise disenfranchised from higher education and to adult/older students, as well as to provide education more relevant to employers. But based on my own memories of trends in the late 1990s and early 2000s, I can confirm that Noble's concerns and fears about the rise of traditional/contemporary courses in both the proprietary market and more traditional universities were widespread in academia. There was indeed concern about the partnerships Noble so vehemently criticizes and the rise and subsequent further corporatization of institutions like the University of Phoenix. As Gary Chapman (1998) wrote, "Faculties have many reasons to be alarmed by such trends, of course. The ultimate realization of 'virtual universities' would be a market-driven panoply of courses offered by 'stars' in each respective field, eroding the need for depth in university faculties and fostering a kind of celebrity hierarchy driven by profit."

Simultaneously, many universities (including the one where I work) were trying to capture a part of the rising online higher education

market for themselves, the theory being that our online degree pro-
grams could be accessible to any student anywhere in the world. In a *New
York Times* article by Karen Arenson (1998), Penn State vice president
James H. Ryan said, "This is the hottest and most sweeping development
I've ever seen. It's like being on a roller coaster; it's a thrill a minute."

While Noble warns his readers of the dangers of corporate partnerships with the rise of traditional/contemporary online courses and
programs, he also describes these partnerships' downfalls and failures.
Onlinelearning.net lost $2 million in its first year. Universities quickly
discovered that most of the "'distance learning' customers"—the
hypothesized students taking courses from hundreds or thousands of
miles away who would increase enrollments and pay more tuition—were
actually traditional students usually on campus, and retention rates in
online courses were significantly lower than those in traditional courses
(Noble 2001, 57). Perhaps the most damning evidence of the down-
fall of these corporate partnerships is the fact that all of the ones I've
mentioned so far—THEN, Onlinelearning.net, and UNNEXT.com—no
longer exist.

There have also been some successes at odds with Noble's warnings.
Online institutions, degrees, and courses have become an accepted and
normal means of delivery in higher education now—thus my label of
traditional/contemporary—though many of these institutions face an
uncertain future. The nonprofit Western Governors University had a
rocky start ("Expecting an initial enrollment of 5000, WGU enrolled
only 10 people, and received just 75 inquiries" [Noble 2001, 57]), but by
2018 its enrollments had reached almost 100,000 students. In contrast,
enrollments at the once seemingly unstoppable for-profit University of
Phoenix (it had almost 470,000 students in 2010) had "slid to 130,000
students by 2016. And last year the university closed 20 of its campus
locations and laid off hundreds of employees" (McKenzie 2018).

Further, traditional/contemporary online courses are now a part of
the mix of delivery methods at almost all traditional universities in the
United States. According to a 2015 report, 95 percent of institutions
with more than 5,000 students offer courses defined as "distant offerings" (which generally means online courses but also includes other
nontraditional formats) (Allen and Seaman 2015). A 2012 report from
the US Department of Education's National Center for Education
Statistics on enrollment in distance education courses indicated that of
the 19 million undergraduate and graduate students enrolled in public
and private nonprofit colleges and universities in the United States,
1.7 million are enrolled exclusively in distance education courses and

2.7 million are enrolled in at least some distance education courses ("Enrollment in Distance Education Courses, by State: Fall 2012" 2014). Clay Shirky (2015) observed that "at the current rate of growth, half the country's undergraduates will have at least one online class on their transcripts by the end of the decade."

Ultimately, Noble's dire warnings about the threat posed by online universities and partnerships between nonprofit educational institutions and for-profit educational entrepreneurs have not proven to be accurate. Like the Flexner versus Bittner and Mallory debate over correspondence courses, the definition of what subjects are worthy of study in universities and what ought to be confined to vocational training has always been shifting. Like Flexner, Noble seems to me to set too stark a contrast between "training" and "education," and he fails to acknowledge the ways alternatives to traditional university courses are valuable. We should be concerned about the rise of for-profit companies in higher education, but we also have to recognize that the track records of these companies in the past (and in the present with the fading of MOOC providers like Coursera and Udacity) in higher education have been poor. On the other hand, I think Noble was raising important questions about the potential problems that result from partnerships between nonprofit institutions and the for-profit companies they hire to market, develop, and even teach online programs and courses. This is a concern I'll return to in the last chapter in discussing the rise of so-called Online Program Management firms.

But again, despite reports and catchy TED talk introductions to the contrary, neither innovation in the delivery of education nor MOOCs are new. The cycle of the "next big thing" to disrupt higher education is at least 125 years old at this stage, and there is no reason to believe we have seen the end of this hype. The incredibly rapid rise and fall of MOOCs makes it difficult to determine how they will be remembered relative to these earlier inventions, but make no mistake that MOOCs have a place within this well-documented historical context.

# 3
## MOOCS IN THE STUDENT CONTEXT

Before I began to study MOOCs, I was a MOOC student, enrolling in and completing my first MOOC in the summer of 2012. Eventually, my MOOC student experiences transformed into scholarship and expertise, which is what led me to the works I've published and edited about MOOCs, along with this book.

This chapter is my story about what it was like to engage in MOOCs as a student. I recognize the scholarly limitations of this perspective. This chapter is "just my story." My interactions with other MOOC students were limited, and I did not try to contact or interview other students. Even if Coursera or the other providers had granted me more access for this project (I didn't ask), the work of securing the proper permissions through my university's Institutional Review Board would have probably been impossible, and, ideally, this kind of research is approved by an IRB *before* it begins, which wasn't my experience here.

So, my approach in this chapter is as an "autoethnographer." As the word might suggest, autoethnography is an ethnography of the self. It's a method Deborah E. Reed-Danahay (1997, 2) describes that "synthesizes both a postmodern ethnography, in which the realist conventions and objective observer position of standard ethnography have been called into question, and a postmodern autobiography, in which the notion of the coherent, individual self has been similarly called into question." As is clear throughout Reed-Danahay's collection of essays, a variety of competing notions and methods fall under the umbrella term *autoethnography*. But for my purposes, I mean something more akin to what Heewon Chang (2008, 43) describes: "Autoethnography shares the storytelling feature with other genres of self-narrative but transcends mere narration of self to engage in cultural analysis and interpretation."

I wasn't the only MOOC scholar who used an autoethnographic approach to such research. Melanie James (2017) describes her own methods and experiences as a MOOC autoethnographer, and she, too, acknowledges that autoethnography is "a contested research approach,"

DOI: 10.7330/9781607327875.c003

one in which "academic rigour is often questioned." In the face of such criticism, "Autoethnographers might be considered somewhat stupid to even attempt their projects. Or maybe they are brave in trying to explore different approaches to exploring social phenomena in which they themselves are involved. From my perspective it feels like a bit of both" (James 2017, 83).

While I don't quote my fellow MOOC students' essays or discussion posts, I do quote liberally from the anonymous student comments I received on the writing assignments I completed because these were comments *I* received as a student and were a part of *my* experiences as a MOOC student. I also quote myself extensively from previous writings on my blog, stevendkrause.com, and from articles and chapters I've previously published. It's a bit awkward to cite myself, but much like an ethnographer's thick notebook, I think the reflections I wrote while in the midst of the MOOCs are valuable in understanding my student experience.

## BEGINNING WITH "LISTENING TO WORLD MUSIC"

By late spring 2012, I was reading and blogging about MOOCs generally, and I had signed up for and participated inconsistently in Curtis J. Bonk's "Empowering Learning through Community," a MOOC offered through Blackboard "designed to provide both theoretical concepts and practical tools for instructors to improve motivation, retention, and engagement within blended and online courses" (Kim 2012). Bonk is a professor of instructional systems technology in the School of Education at Indiana University, has published extensively about online pedagogy, and (with Mimi M. Lee, Thomas C. Reeves, and Thomas H. Reynolds) edited the collection *MOOCs and Open Education around the World* (2015). Curiously, one of the distinguishing characteristics of Bonk's 2012 MOOC was that it was one of the first high-profile/high-enrollment MOOCs that was organized by someone with previous expertise in online pedagogy. I drifted in and out of the course, not exactly wowed by the experience, though I think that was as much my problem as anything else. Bonk's approach included solid advice and useful materials for those who had never taught online before, but since I had been teaching online for several years, I found the course too basic for my needs.

I was skeptical but still curious about MOOCs, and by July 2012 the mainstream and educational media hype about them was increasing. Certainly, MOOCs weren't something to forget quite yet. So in late July 2012, I enrolled in the first MOOC I completed, Coursera's "Listening to World Music." (While the archive of "Listening to World Music" was accessible as late as 2015, it has since been removed by Coursera.) I decided to sign up for the course because it seemed to me to be a good balance of something I was interested in and capable of learning more about without being too far out of my comfort zone. "Listening to World Music" seemed just about right.

"Listening to World Music" was a seven-week MOOC taught by Carol Muller, who is a professor of music at the University of Pennsylvania specializing in ethnomusicology. Based on what she reports on her website, Muller has been a professor at UPenn since 2008, and she is clearly an accomplished scholar and teacher. She is South African, and most of her scholarship seems to be about the music of that region. Her CV also suggests that Muller had had previous experience teaching online courses at UPenn and in a community outreach program called West Philadelphia Music. (I reached out via email to Muller and her teaching assistants several times to ask if they would be willing to participate as case study interview subjects about their experiences teaching the MOOC, but they never answered.)

When the course first began, we were told there were about 20,000 students from all over the world (that number would ultimately grow to 36,000). I was surprised initially by the apparatus around the course that made it all seem very much like "college." There was an honor code agreement and a syllabus that outlined the requirements as if it were just another Gen Ed/lecture hall class. This presumption of MOOC students being just like other college students was a common misunderstanding of early MOOC providers, which is surprising considering the hopes of Koller and the like to reach a global audience. As Rebecca Bennett and Mike Kent noted (2017, 15), these early MOOC providers "designed the online courses with the assumption that MOOC students would be familiar with the discourses, tropes and cultures associated with, if not a specific discipline, Western-based university culture as a whole." Reading over the syllabus, I was looking forward to some of the topics of the course, and it reminded me of the music appreciation college course I took twenty-five years ago.

There were basically two forms of teaching delivered in the course. First, there was Muller doing a traditional lecture: talking from notes that she glanced at once in a while, standing in front of a black background and looking directly into one camera, with black-and-white slides over her shoulder. The lectures were broken into 10–15-minute segments with links to YouTube clips of music examples. As I wrote on my blog back in late July 2012: "It's all so simple and mundane on so many different levels. Coursera is supposed to 'revolutionize' the way teaching works, and what we have here is a 'sage on the stage' and [a] completely non-interactive lecture that has the production values of a small midwestern town's public access television station. This, *this* is going to 'blow away 99% of classes available at traditional colleges?' Really?" (http://stevendkrause.com/2012/07/27/going-back-to-school -mooc-style-starting-world-music/).

I wasn't the only one taking "Listening to World Music" who felt similarly about these issues. Tamara Lewin of the *New York Times* was also a student in the course. While she generally praised the course, she also said "the production values were pitiful, with the professor displaying photos too small to see of her gumboot dancing time in South Africa or gesticulating like an inexperienced weatherman trying to point to the correct area on a map" (Lewin 2012).

The other teaching delivery method was a series of videos of Muller's graduate assistants for the course discussing that week's lectures and music. These are hard to describe because I had not seen this approach to online teaching before this course, and I haven't seen it again in any of the other MOOCs I've taken. But essentially, groups of two or three graduate students sat on a couch in front of a green screen image—usually of a college courtyard or some other outdoor scene—and enthusiastically and energetically discussed Muller's lectures and the music for that week. They seemed to take the form of an idealized small-group session, like the discussion sections led by GAs that often accompany large lecture hall classes such as this one in more traditional face-to-face settings.

I blogged about these graduate student–led discussions a bit off and on, particularly during the third week of the course. My fellow MOOC students' reactions to these videos (as posted in the discussion forums) were divided:

> One is "Appreciation for the Grad student discussions! THANKS to the grads!" while the other is "Pretentious grad student talk vs live seminar with actual classmates." I posted to both threads. In the "Appreciation" thread, I suggested that both the grad students and Muller need to spend a lot more time practicing their presentation skills and making something more interesting than just people talking at us. That one got two "negative" votes. On the "Pretentious" thread, I posted about how the format is all wrong—these talks are pre-recorded, and they aren't the same interaction as the students because they're talking head videos instead of words typed in a forum. I suggested that they record these grad student conversations live in a way as to actually answer student questions. This post got two "positive" votes and some "great idea" rejoinders from Coursera "staff"/ grad students. (http://stevendkrause.com/2012/08/13/mooc-week/)

The certificate or "statement of accomplishment" for the course was based on completing six of seven short writing assignments and earning at least a 70 percent grade on a final exam. I discuss this aspect of the class in some detail in my contribution to a "Symposium on Massive Open Online Courses" that appeared in the June 2013 issue of *College Composition and Communication*. Interestingly, the MOOC that was the subject of the other contribution to this symposium, by Jeff Rice, was also "Listening to World Music."

Each week, we were given a choice of four 500-word writing prompts. For example, the topic of the second week of the MOOC was Paul Simon's album "*Graceland*, a World Music Collaboration?" As a good academic, Muller's approach here was to problematize the politics surrounding the production and the "double, and opposite meanings of the word 'appropriate.'" After beginning with an introductory lecture about the album that highlighted the songs "Boy in the Bubble" and "Homeless," Muller expanded on the South African political context of Apartheid and the album *Sun City: Artists United against Apartheid*, along with more details about the choral singing style Isicathamiya (made famous in America on Simon's album with the group Ladysmith Black Mambazo) and gumboot dancing. Of the four options available this week, I decided to write about this prompt: "Take a look at the 'Graceland' album as a whole, presented on the Paul Simon website or on other commercial sites. Do you think 'collaboration' is an appropriate description of how this album was created, and who has benefited most from its sales and global distribution? Is it possible for there to be a fair and equitable process of musical exchange (as Malm portrays in the first sketch of global musical encounters) between so called 'first' and 'third' world musicians? Who benefited most artistically, creatively, and financially from this project? Always provide reasons for your speculation or position."

My response was more than 500 words divided into four paragraphs, and it contained a long quote from a *USA Today* article about the twenty-fifth anniversary of the album's original release. In any event, the routine here was to submit the assignment for peer assessment by the stated deadline.

Before I describe the second step of the process generally, an important tangent here about a missed deadline for this particular assignment. There was a technical snafu with Coursera that caused this submission—the second of the course—to be technically "late." The result was that my grade on the assignment was docked 20 percent. I was bothered by this, of course, and there was quite a bit of complaining from other students on the site. As I wrote on my blog when this happened: "WTF?!?! And *then* it turned out that (a) I wasn't the only one who was annoyed/confused at the deduction since this was never explained anywhere, and (b) there was some sort of technical glitch in the Coursera software that caused this to happen in the first place." Later in that same post I wrote:

> I don't want to make too much of a big deal out of this because I know these things are all experimental, not really for credit, free, new, etc. And I have nothing at all against the premise of peer evaluation for these projects, though in a "real class" setting I suspect there might be some FERPA [Family Education Rights and Privacy Act] objections, a lot of students expressed some anxiety at the idea of grading their peers, and I'd like to see a much more robust rubric/evaluation technology . . . But I think this little bump points to one of the problems of scaling classes to tens of thousands. A lot of people were kind of irritated by this in a class that is completely free and where the stakes are very low; imagine what would happen if students enrolled had to score a certain number to be potentially eligible to take a CLEP [College Level Examination Program]–styled test to get real credit. Worse yet, imagine if someone had actually paid *real money* for this! (http://stevendkrause.com/2012/08/06/more-moocines/, original, emphasis)

Because there was no way for Muller and her small group of graduate assistants to read and assess these writing assignments, the grading of these short writings was "crowdsourced" to the students in the class through the peer review process. The Coursera course management system randomly assigned each of us three to five other student writing responses to read and evaluate based on a specific rubric. The rubric had five criteria:

- Style
- Does It Address the Question?
- Strength of the Argument
- Integration of Personal Response to Music with Critical Thought
- Relevance to Large Course Themes

For each of these, the scoring was 0, 1, or 2. As I wrote in my article in *College Composition and Communication*, the rubric was initially presented to students with no guidelines, examples, or explanation as to what each of these criterion meant or what the appropriate score meant. So, for example, take "Does It Address the Question?"

- A "0" score meant "No, or barely. This response could be completely off-topic, or it could be almost entirely tangential."
- A "1" score meant "Sort of. This response might meander around the *topic* without addressing the *question*" (original emphasis).

- A "2" score meant "Yes. This response gets straight to the heart of the question, and it is clear why any external comparisons are pertinent." (http://spark-public.s3.amazonaws.com/worldmusic/Rubric/WorldMusicRubric.pdf)

In terms of the grading scale, this is how I described my approach in the *CCC*: "I suppose the logic was to allow each assignment to be worth an even 10 points, but for me, a 0 meant the writer did nothing at all, so in practice, I gave my peers either a 1 or a 2 on each item. And because the criteria themselves were so poorly defined and never discussed, what I found myself doing was simply assigning 1's and 2's to each item with a fuzzy notion of 'okay' equaling 1 point and 'good' equaling 2" (Krause 2013, 692). While there was a fair amount of discussion on the class site about these writing assignments and good examples from students, I didn't find any discussion about the rubric or the grading scale.

I submitted my work and then reviewed the work of my peers. My work as a peer reviewer was weak, perhaps because of the dubious grading scale and the lack of accountability (the quality of my work as a reviewer had no impact on my earning a certificate in the course), or perhaps as a writing teacher I do enough of this sort of work and simply didn't want to do any more.

For the first week's assignment (I earned a 10), I had three peer reviews. The first said I made some excellent points but added, "I think you could possibly work on writing in a more academic and formal style." My second reviewer said my response was well-written but that I should have elaborated "a bit on the aspects of the music itself," and my third reviewer said I had made them "think about the issue of commodification." These are all engaging comments, though I couldn't follow up with the reviewers since the process was doubly anonymous: that is, I didn't know who they were, and they didn't know who I was. That's a shame, since this was an opportunity for more interaction. Asking the first two reviewers what they meant by their comments could have potentially helped me think differently about my writing.

For the assignment for week two—the one where I was docked 20 percent since I had supposedly turned in my work late—I earned an 8 and minimal feedback from only two peers. During week three, I found myself busy with all the things I needed to do besides this MOOC, and, after sympathizing for a moment with my own students who I often forget have other things to do in their lives besides my class, I dashed off a quick and haphazard prompt. I earned a 9 and again minimal feedback from only two peers—though interestingly, one of those peers noted "you have left 54% of your word limit unused."

By about the fourth week of the course, I was getting a little bored with the content. Muller was emphasizing music I wasn't that interested in, and the course (as I wrote in my blog) was "starting to feel more and more like I went to a music class and an anthropology/sociology class decided to barge in and take things over" (http://stevendkrause.com /2012/08/25/mooc-week-five-and-the-peer-review-turns/). So, partly as a result of that boredom and partly because of my own curiosity, I tried what I described on my blog as a "slip-shot/half-assed" experiment. Here's a lengthy quote from the *CCC* symposium article describing what I did and the results:

> For the first three weeks, I took the assignments seriously and completed them earnestly. But for the fourth week's writing assignment, I decided to test the process a bit. In response to a prompt about "Pygmy" traditional music and free culture, I began with a paragraph that was connected to the prompt and some of my own reading and research on "open source" scholarship. The second paragraph began with a related tangent about Disney's problematic relationship to free culture, and then it slipped into a few sentences I copied and pasted from one of my blog posts—that is, sentences clearly out of nowhere and plagiarized (albeit self-plagiarized). My concluding paragraph circled back to the original topic, though it was hastily put together.
>
> I earned an 8.5 out of 10, and I think the two written responses I received from peers speak volumes to the diversity of my fellow students. The first response was almost 300 words long and had the voice of an experienced first-year writing teacher. This peer complimented me on my opening paragraph but then noted my "second paragraph was, however, highly problematic: it seemed like you're missing some citations here." The peer went on: "Because of this disjointed incoherence, I did a quick google search of those sentences that didn't seem appropriate," and this reviewer included a link to my blog post that had been the source of my self-plagiarism. The peer critiqued my third paragraph for making "two huge claims . . . without any support for either of them," and then concluded: "I still gave you a pretty high score, only marking off for 'relevant to larger course themes,' but I thought you could have taken this essay further than you did."
>
> In contrast, the second peer's entire response read: "Good work. Some chill out music for you http://youtu.be/ccqY-R_M2nY." The link is to a song titled "Bug Powder Dust" by a techno/dance/remix one-person band called "Bomb the Bass."
>
> Obviously, there are several problems here. The first student was far too engaged in the process, and the second student was hardly engaged at all, though for all I know, my second peer reviewer may have thought he or she was doing an excellent job with this review. Perhaps sharing some "chill-out music" was something my second reviewer thought was key to the process. Without any meaningful intervention or interaction from an instructor, who is to say? And even the first student, who put a lot of work

in discussing the problems of my response, still ended up giving me a good grade. (Krause 2013, 693–694)

Muller, her graduate assistants, and the staff at Coursera looking in on the course must have noted similar kinds of problems in the peer evaluation process because in week six of the course (the last week of writing assignments), these instructions were added to the "Overall evaluation/ feedback" section of the rubric: "To be fair to your peers you are required to provide some rationale/justification for the grade you give for their assignment. Provide between 5 and 100 words in the space below."

In addition to the short writing exercises, the final "grade" for "Listening to World Music" was a multiple choice and comprehensive exam, which was the work of the last week of the course (rather than a writing assignment). Here is how I wrote about it on my blog:

> I got a 73. I didn't exactly study for this test and I am sure some simple review of the stuff we had done before would have probably helped my score quite a bit. It was also a test fairly easy to cheat on [and] take advantage of the open book/open note format of things. I had plenty of time to do some Google searches for some of the questions that were stumping me, and if I had thought about it ahead of time, I probably could have opened up parts of the course in another browser to look stuff up as I was taking the test. Plus, if I'm understanding things right, it appears that I could even retake the exam if I wanted to, which seems like quite the advantage, especially if I had saved the original exam. (http://stevendkrause.com/ 2012/09/11/the-end-of the world-music-mooc-part-1/)

The other ongoing element of the course was the discussion forums. Similar to other online courses and online bulletin board spaces, the forums were threaded discussions that were divided up based on the week of the course and on headlines for beginnings of discussions. Some of the discussions were initiated by the course organizers and instructors, and some were initiated by students. It was very similar to the kind of threaded discussions common in more conventional online courses, but with the larger and more chaotic tinge of the discussions I frequently see in the comment sections of newspaper websites. The most apt (and clichéd) comparison I can make is like drinking from a fire hose: so many people talking about so many different things simply did not lend itself to any particularly useful interaction. I tried to participate off and on as the course went along, but ultimately, I gave up on the discussions entirely. I think Rice (2013, 700) captured the feel of the discussion forums well in his *CCC* article:

> A forum question regarding access to peer assessments at a reasonable hour for those living outside of the United States went unanswered

by the course professor and graduate assistants. The thread eventually drifted into a discussion of women's cycling and swimming in the Olympics. Another thread asking participants to add their own playlist of music based on their own geography offered new material worth viewing, though not in connection with course content . . . The most lively discussion I may have encountered regarded the two- to three-paragraph requirement, a requirement questioned by many students as not enough space for expression. No resolution was reached. My second choice for lively discussion might be a thread on whether or not Cuba is run by a dictatorship. Its exigency was a side comment made during one of the professor's lectures. The thread drifted far off from course content.

As chaotic as the discussion forums were, they actually weren't used by many, at least relative to the size and scale of the course. At the closing of "Listening to World Music" in September 2012, I received (presumably along with all of the other course participants) an email with some basic and interesting statistics about student interaction with the course. The email stated that 36,295 users registered for the course, and 3,859 users were active in the last week of the course, which means that about 90 percent of users were no longer active by the end—though I'm hesitant to describe these missing users as "dropouts" since I suspect many of them never "dropped-in" to the course in the first place. There were 17,339 posts in the discussion forums for the course. On average, that means about 4.5 posts per user, though that average doesn't tell much of the story. In addition to the fact that many of those posts were from the teaching assistants and staff associated with the course (for example, one of the most present and active teaching assistants for the course had 342 forum posts), it also doesn't account for the same phenomenon of a few students who wrote dozens and dozens of posts. In other words, it would appear that the discussion space for "Listening to World Music" has the classic "long tail" distribution of users in which a very small number of participants account for the vast majority of content and discussion on the site. That is a model that might work to generate content for sites like Wikipedia, but it is far from ideal for online pedagogy, which is to encourage and require everyone to participate.

Looking back at "Listening to World Music"—now that I've taken a few more MOOCs and time has passed—I think I was too harsh on my blog, perhaps because I was feeling defensive about the threat of MOOCs replacing traditional college instruction. I could not understand how anyone in the mainstream media or anywhere else could possibly imagine MOOCs as a worthy substitute for institutional education. "Listening to World Music" was too incomplete, too much a work in progress. On the other hand, because it was so shaky a work in progress experiment, my defensiveness about the threat of MOOCs now seems ill-placed.

As I noted in my last blog post about "Listening to World Music," the University of Pennsylvania organizers sent all students a last email about the forthcoming certificate of completion that also contained an invitation to participate in a survey about the course. The last question of that survey was "If Penn hosted a World Music Extension experience based on the priorities you selected, what rate (US $) would you be willing to pay to enroll?" The answer space was a sliding scale going from $0 to $500. My answer to that question was "$0." I also wrote this in my blog:

> Judging from what I've seen in the discussion on the Facebook group for the class, I'd say that my answer is in the general price range of my fellow students (though one went as high as $25). In fact, now that I think of it, I'd say that Coursera has more or less the same problem as Facebook: I know lots of people who are wildly enthusiastic and near obsessive users of Facebook, but I don't know anyone who would actually pay for it. Content (aka learning) in and of itself has very little value on the internet. (http://stevendkrause.com/2012/09/14/and-what-did-we-learn-her/)

## EDC MOOC

After finishing "Listening to World Music," my MOOC studies slowed because of my professorial responsibilities. I did spend some time in November 2012 in the MOOC "Introduction to Genetics and Evolution." It was taught by Mohamed Noor, a professor of biology at Duke University specializing in genetics. Noor's approach in the MOOC is what I described in my blog as "very straight-forward /old-school" in that he gave lectures, there were problems assigned with due dates, and that was about it. There were discussion forums, but as far as I could tell, they seemed an afterthought.

I didn't spend enough time with the class to describe it in any detail, but I did make a couple of observations about Noor's approach: "The plus-side of Mohamed Noor: he's a good lecturer who has clearly given these kinds of talks in front of a camera before. He's comfortable—almost too comfortable. I think the 'production values' and format are better than in 'Listening to World Music' in that they are more Khan-academy style: it's a white board-esque presentation that Noor annotates as he talks, and while he is still present as a talking head, he's off in the corner" (http://stevendkrause.com/2012/11/04/more-on-moocs/). But the downside, as I saw it, was that the "class philosophy" page on the Coursera site made it very clear that Noor "freely (with no compensation) donated his time to producing this course," and because he was essentially alone in running the course, students shouldn't expect any response from him. I found this disappointing, and I wrote: "First off, the idea that Noor has 'donated his time' is a wee-bit problematic from my point of view, mainly because I do the work I do not out of the goodness of my heart but because I get paid. I certainly wouldn't donate my time to Coursera like this. Second, if you are explicitly not available to students, then you aren't an 'instructor;' rather, you're more of a presenter or author, which is why I think MOOCs are a lot more like textbooks than classes" (http://stevendkrause.com/2012/11/04/more-on-moocs/).

I'll return to these issues in chapter 4 in terms of successful "performances" online, the unsustainability of a teaching model where faculty teach a course with no compensation, and this connection between MOOCs and textbooks. But for now, I want to say two other things, more or less in Noor's defense. First, Noor actually *was* a lot more available than his class philosophy might have suggested, and he was one of the first MOOC instructors I saw who tried to make connections with MOOC students in real time. In this case, Noor participated in a Google Hangout discussion, though (as is often the case with first-time users of this kind of conferencing software) a lot of the discussion seemed to be about the forum itself—as in "hey, we're on Google Hangout."

Second, Noor took what he has learned from the MOOC experience and applied it to a "flipped classroom" approach to teaching his Duke lecture hall courses, as he wrote about on his blog *Science, Food, Etc.* (Noor 2013). In other words, while Noor claimed to have "volunteered" his time in teaching his MOOC (and he might still hold to that claim), the reality is that his experiences in teaching a MOOC have clearly been part of his professional development in his more traditional teaching.

At this point my MOOC experiences as a student merged with my teaching responsibilities. During the winter 2013 semester at EMU, I taught a graduate course called "Computers and Writing, Theory and Practice," a requirement for students in our Masters in Written Communications program pursuing a specialization in the teaching of writing. The course—besides obviously being about computers and writing—is also a writing pedagogy course concerned with the connections between teaching and technology. So, with all the hype surrounding MOOCs, I decided to include a significant unit on MOOCs for the course. The other interesting wrinkle with this section of "Computers and Writing" was that it was offered online. Like most graduate seminars, it was a small group (it started with only nine students), I knew all of the students from previous courses and work on campus, and there were a number of optional but well-attended face-to-face experiences to talk about the course materials. So, while the course was asynchronous and online, there was a bit of a hybrid feel to it in that everyone was familiar with everyone else in real life.

I previously wrote about this course and my experiences in the essay "MOOC Assigned" and also in an essay called "Always Alone and Together: Three of My MOOC Student Discussion and Participation Experiences" (Krause 2014, 2017). As I wrote in the opening paragraphs of "MOOC Assigned," by this time I had started seeing the potential of MOOCs not so much as *courses* per se but as textbooks for courses. "After all," I wrote, "textbooks are mass produced collections of content created and assembled by experts (and often notable scholars) of the field with particular pedagogical strategies and courses in mind, which are then used by other instructors who usually do not have the level of expertise as the textbook authors" (Krause 2014, 122). My goal for my graduate course was to assign students to participate in a MOOC about teaching and technology, both as an experience of "inhabiting" a MOOC and also to learn from the subject matter of the MOOC itself.

The MOOC I chose for the course was "E-Learning and Digital Cultures" (EDC MOOC), which was hosted by Coursera and team-taught by Sian Bayne, Jeremy Knox, Hamish Macleod, Jen Ross, and Christine Sinclair, all of whom were faculty or graduate students in the MSc in Digital Education program at the University of Edinburgh. I first learned about the program at Edinburgh and this MOOC through their "Manifesto for Teaching Online" and an article the team had written about their upcoming MOOC in the *ALT Online Newsletter* (Knox et al. 2012). In that article Knox and colleagues spoke frankly about the problems with xMOOCs. They saw too much "digital mimicry," where online courses were trying to "justify their status by promoting curricula that are equivalent to campus-based courses," and they expressed concern that the huge enrollments in MOOCs were accompanied by equally huge dropout rates (Knox et al. 2012). They also expressed a concern I had had with my previous MOOCs, the rarefaction of the "superstar" professor at the center of it all:

> The persona of the course tutor can become more that of a celebrity with an almost talismanic status than a present, real teacher. In our conventional online teaching we've worked hard to maintain and build the role of the teacher in the face of a tendency—driven by a sometimes uncritical emphasis on learner-centredness—to push the role into the background. So we are keen to avoid both the over-celebratory fetishizing of the teacher associated with some MOOCs, and the tendency to see the technology

as allowing us to write the teacher out of the equation altogether. We want to explore how a MOOC pedagogy might work with a construction of the teacher that has an immediacy that can succeed at scale. (Knox et al. 2012)

So, in working with Coursera (the University of Edinburgh had earlier entered into a partnership with them), the team behind the EDC MOOC was able to test and demonstrate on a very large scale some of the theses it had metaphorically nailed to the Web in 2011 in its "Manifesto for Teaching Online." Some examples from the twenty-point manifesto included:

- The possibility of the "online version" is overstated. The best online courses are born digital.
- Every course design is philosophy and belief in action.
- Assessment strategies can be designed to allow for the possibility of resistance. ("Manifesto for Teaching Online" 2011)

Like all manifestos, these claims were meant to provoke debate and not resolve it, but I did find myself agreeing with the sentiment and the general claims. I was also intrigued by the possibility of how this manifesto arguing for openness and experimentation in distance education might come to be realized within the closed shell of a Coursera MOOC.

EDC MOOC began at the same time as the course I was teaching, and my graduate students and I jumped into the course with a lot of excitement and apprehension about how this was going to work. As I wrote in "MOOC Assigned," "We were the rats in the maze and simultaneously the scientists watching how that rat negotiated the turns" (Krause 2014, 123). Further, I had assigned this particular MOOC more or less blind; that is, beyond the description of the course and an educated guess (based on the group's online teaching manifesto), I wasn't sure how the course would play out.

At the start of EDC MOOC, none of my students had previous MOOC experience, and their initial concerns about the MOOC dwelled on this lack of familiarity with the format—natural enough worries. As the professor and someone more familiar with MOOCs, I was worried about two different aspects of the course: "First, while the description of the course strongly implied an emphasis on pedagogy, the real emphasis was on digital cultures, with the major units focusing on utopias and dystopias and humanism (along with post-humanism and anti-humanism)" (Krause 2014, 124). This did not represent a significant disconnect from the subject of my course—it certainly was closer in terms of content than a MOOC about music or genetics would have been—but there wasn't as much reading and discussion specifically about teaching as I had anticipated.

Second, the format of EDC MOOC was a clear and intentional departure from the previous MOOCs I'd taken and read about. There were no "talking head" lecture videos, and the metaphor of a lecture hall course was completely dismissed. The team behind EDC MOOC was trying to run what George Siemens (2012b) dubbed a "connectivist MOOC" in that this MOOC was more focused on networking, creation, creativity, and autonomy. This alternative approach in teaching wasn't that surprising given the group's manifesto, and I understood why the EDC MOOC took this tack. Nonetheless, because this was a departure from the "norm" for MOOCs (at least of the previous MOOCs I had taken), it wasn't necessarily the best example for my students.

EDC MOOC moved quickly—it was a five-week course—and my online class moved quickly along with it. My students seemed to like the content of the course, but they also felt the conscious absence of faculty went too far. Because most of these students were progressing through our MA program's emphasis on the teaching of writing, they were already familiar with the key assumptions of the field that I discuss in the introduction—that "writing is a process" and the ideal setting for a "student-centered" classroom is a small one where students' work and activities are the primary focus as opposed to a lecture-based, "sage on the stage" approach to teaching. But the consensus among my students a couple of weeks into the class was that writing "student-centered" didn't mean "teacher-absent." They were also concerned about and confused by the disorganized stream of thousands of other students in the discussion forums, and my students noted several times that this could be mitigated by dividing the course into smaller sections.

I shared a lot of these thoughts and wrote about them on my blog in late February 2013, roughly the halfway point of the course:

> Interestingly enough, one of the better discussion threads is in the general discussion area and it's called "Where are the professors?" (I presume the only way to see that is to actually be in the class, but if you're curious, there's nothing wrong with registering for free and then going to have a look.) The topic of the role of the professor in a MOOC is being debated and a couple of the instructors—Christine Sinclair and Sian Bayne—are pretty clear in responding that they are attempting to avoid the "guru professor" mode and are purposefully trying to present themselves as being more of a "connective MOOC" rather than the so-called "xMOOC" which is the commercial model of Coursera. http://stevendkrause.com/2013/02/18/halfway-through-edcmooc-whatever-it-is/

There were two general problems with this approach. First, as mentioned, the Coursera assumption in its learning management system was of the "guru professor" mode the EDC MOOC team was trying to avoid, and those problems showed in the clunkiness of the discussion forums. Second, the highly de-centered nature of EDC MOOC meant it was not really a "course." Neither one of these issues was exactly a problem for the EDC MOOC team so much as they were concerns for me and my students, especially since we were approaching EDC MOOC as part of the traditional online course I was teaching—a course considerably more structured, gradable, and certifiable than EDC MOOC.

Ultimately, I was disappointed with EDC MOOC—not as disappointed as my cheeky blog post titled "E-Learning and Digital Cultures Ends with a Meh" might suggest, but disappointed nonetheless. The content of the course wasn't what my students and I were promised, and it was inconsistent. Some of the readings were on-point and provoked lively discussions in my online class, while other readings were either over the heads of my graduate students or too elementary for even a first-year–level course. The absence of the faculty—while clearly in line with the EDC MOOC group's "manifesto" for online teaching—went too far, at least if EDC MOOC was to be counted as a "course," which is perhaps part of the problem. In the course of blogging about EDC MOOC in 2013, I came across a post on Sandra K. Milligan's blog titled "Better than a Tarantino Movie: Raw Peer Assessment in #edcmooc," in which she addresses these issues. Milligan is a department member in education at the University of Melbourne and a fellow EDC MOOC student. In her end of the course review on her blog, she wrote: "In retrospect, it might have been better to market the course as an 'online extended conference' or 'a discussion group' or, as Hamish Macleod, one of the team members wryly put it in the first hangout, a good old 1970s-style 'happening.' As a course it was a great happening. How to assess a happening, or how to structure a happening into a course are the questions I would turn to for next time" (Milligan 2013).

I did discover some changes to later versions of EDC MOOC that seemed to respond to these disconnections. While preparing my chapter for the Losh collection, I re-enrolled in the fall 2014 version of the class. The readings and discussion forums appeared to be similar, but this version of the course included video introductions to the five units, each featuring one of the five faculty leading the course. The videos were shot at different locations on and near the University of Edinburgh's campus, and, as I wrote in "Always Alone and Together," "The videos have the look of a nationally syndicated public television show, professionally produced with multiple scene changes while the well rehearsed and focused voiceovers from the professors continue. These videos were short—the longest one just over five minutes—and they end with questions designed to help lead students through that week's discussion" (Krause 2017, 248). In other words, EDC MOOC hadn't surrendered and shoved the "sages" back onto the stage, but it at least acknowledged the presence of teachers to help frame the discussion.

## ENGLISH COMPOSITION 1: ACHIEVING EXPERTISE

"English Composition 1: Achieving Expertise" is the only MOOC I took that was squarely in my own area of expertise of composition and rhetoric. When I began the course, I didn't know the professor who taught and developed it, Denise Comer, but academic disciplines tend to be very small worlds. As I wrote on my blog, "I hesitate in being too critical and I apologize up front if I'm too negative, and Denise, if you're reading this, let's introduce ourselves to each other at some conference or something and I'll buy you a beer regardless of how you feel about my commentary" (http://stevendkrause.com/2013/03/27 /week-1-in-dukes-english-1-mooc/). As I write this now, I'm happy to report that I have gotten to know Denise a bit through this MOOC, through the chapter she contributed to *Invasion of the MOOCs*, and through the interview I conducted with her that I discuss in chapter 4. While I don't think we necessarily agree about MOOCs or this course, my awkwardness now is perhaps that I know her too well. Though I have yet to buy her a beer.

"English Composition 1" was similar to the previous Coursera MOOCs I had taken: the same basic layout of the website/learning platform, the same discussion forums, and similarly modest production values in the "talking head" lecture videos. But Comer, her faculty development partners at Duke, and notable scholars in the field—including Edward White, who is recognized as an expert in writing assessment, and Paul Kei Matsuda, who is director of second language learning at Arizona State University—clearly had learned from past MOOCs. While still chaotic, the discussion forums were much better organized than previous MOOCs I had experienced. While MOOCs always attract many participants from around the world, and I had no actual access to enrollment data at the time the course was running, I sensed a heavy presence in "English Composition 1" of participants for whom English was a second language and also who were somewhat younger than I had experienced in past MOOCs.

My impressions were backed up in scholarship after the course. In February 2016, Comer and White published "Adventuring into MOOC Writing Assessment: Challenges, Results, and Possibilities" in *College Composition and Communication*. They reported that almost 80 percent of participants lived outside the United States, and "77% indicated that English was not their first language" (Comer and White 2016, 320).

Early on, I also noted two intertwined limitations of the experience of "English Composition 1," limitations I don't think the course overcame. First, most of Comer's videos consisted of her delivering lectures. Quite frankly, that's boring—and I say this not only as someone who has taught composition and rhetoric courses for a long time but also as someone who has given plenty of boring lectures. Further, as the course went on, the textbook-like lectures seemed to become less relevant to the actual writing that was being assigned in the course.

Another closely related limitation posed a bigger problem: thousands of participants. MOOCs like "Listening to World Music," "Introduction to Genetics," or even "E-Learning and Digital Cultures" are courses that would probably be successful in a conventional lecture hall format with a professor speaking before a group of 200–300 students, with limited interaction between the professor and students. Writing courses like "English Composition 1" are not taught in a lecture hall format. For me, this speaks to the issue of scalability I noted in chapter 1: MOOCs do not scale for courses we commonly teach in smaller groups, courses where most of the graded work consists of student writing (rather than tests and quizzes where the grading tends to be more automated) and where the interaction between teachers and students is at least as valuable as the expertise conveyed by the professor.

The first of the four main writing assignments for the course was to write a critical review of the first chapter of Daniel Coyle's *The Talent Code*, a book about Coyle's reporting on the source of "talent": where it comes from, how it is cultivated, and so forth. For example, much of this chapter focuses on the unique ways Brazilians grow up learning and practicing soccer. As I wrote in a blog entry, "It's kind of an ironic choice in a way because part of Coyle's point is that talent/expertise comes from 'deep practice,' which isn't exactly the kind of thing that is promoted in a MOOC" (http://stevendkrause.com/2013/04/09/english -composition-i-week-2-and-3/).

One of the more interesting aspects of this reading and the subsequent discussion of it was the fact that Daniel Coyle participated in a video forum discussing his book. Now, there were a variety of technical and production problems with Coyle's participation because of the somewhat finicky synchronous communication technology and also because this was more of a rambling "first come/first served" Q&A session rather than something more structured, such as an interview between Coyle and Comer. Nonetheless, this event did highlight some of the potential of MOOCs generally. If I had assigned the first chapter of *The Talent Code* in my small section of first-year composition, I am quite sure that Coyle would have declined an invitation to attend. In contrast, I assume that the opportunity for Coyle to interact with thousands of readers was both exciting and flattering to him.

Some of the discussion forums were particularly harsh on Coyle, dismissing the reading as simplistic pop psychology/pop journalism. Someone even recommended that a better reading might come from the *Cambridge Handbook of Expertise and Expert Performance*, a 1,000-or-so-page collection of essays with a decidedly more academic bent. Based on my own experiences teaching college freshmen, I believe the readings from Coyle were a more accessible choice. But once again, the suggestions of "better readings" speak to the problem of the range of participants in "English Composition 1," a problem that was also apparent to me with EDC MOOC and every other MOOC I've experimented with: mixing learners with such diverse previous experiences makes it difficult to select readings and exercises presented at a level appropriate for everyone.

I submitted my short essay for peer review, reviewed other peers' essays, and received my feedback. This was similar to the "Listening to World Music" experience in that it was anonymous, though Comer and her colleagues created a rubric specific to the assignment. For example, reviewers were asked to write a response to the following:

- Where in the essay does the author show summary and understanding of Coyle's chapter? Is that sufficient to convey Coyle's main argument to readers who may not have read Coyle?
- Where does the author go beyond summary of the text to pose a question about Coyle's text, raise a limitation about Coyle's argument, or make some other point about Coyle's article?

The review questions less specific to Coyle were still more directed than the prompt for "Listening to World Music" in terms of responding to the draft and in asking the reviewers to reflect on their own work as well:

- What evidence does the writer draw on to support or explicate his or her argument? Has the writer effectively integrated and cited quotes or evidence? If not, say what the writer might do to integrate and cite quotes or evidence more effectively.

- What did you learn about your own writing / your own project based
  on responding to this writer's project?

However, I still found the peer review limiting because I had no chance
to respond to my reviewers or to seek guidance about the feedback I received. This was particularly visible in this specific assignment because
the feedback on my project from my three reviewers was inconsistent.
In a smaller version of a composition course, this is a teachable moment that can lead to a discussion about how writers evaluate reader
feedback in different situations. In a large MOOC, it seems more of a
chance for confusion.

"English Composition 1" continued in this vein. As the course progressed, I saw fewer connections between either the discussions or
Comer's lectures (many of which began to cover more general topics
like plagiarism) and the writing assignments themselves. Finishing the
course proved difficult for me. Part of it was because this was easily
the longest MOOC I enrolled in, and it was also the MOOC that most
resembled a "real" college course in terms of workload. But a lot of the
problem involved how the course fit in with my own teaching work and
how it conflicted with my preparations for summer.

I wasn't the only one who had similar problems. In a series of blog
posts at the *Chronicle of Higher Education*'s "On Hiring" and "The 2
Year Track," Isaac Sweeney wrote about his experiences with "English
Composition 1." He signed up for it earnestly in March, but by early
April he was already worried about being behind and expressing concerns about the format. He wrote: Comer does a "nice job" with the
video lectures, "but it's straight lecture . . . on a prerecorded video. I
can't raise my hand and ask for elaboration. I can't build on a class-
mate's question and engage in an impromptu discussion . . . at least
not during the video" (Sweeney 2013a). In a mid-June post titled "Why
I'm a Bad Student," Sweeney (2013b) explains why he ended up doing
"mostly nothing" with the work of "English Composition 1": he lacked
easy access to high-speed internet connectivity at home, time, money
(Sweeney argued that the class being free was actually a disincentive for
finishing), and "Then, the Other Reasons," which amount to all the life
distractions all of us are vulnerable to—family, "a good game on TV,"
and so forth. John Warner wrote about a similar experience in *Inside
Higher Ed*. Part of his "failure" was similar to mine (we both had our own
student essays to read and grade), and part of it was the sort of illness
that frequently derails my students: "Not sure what it was. Possibly the
plague" (Warner 2013). Also, as I mentioned with my earlier experience

in "Listening to World Music," Warner (2013) did find a new level of empathy for students encountering "some brief misfortune" that can completely disrupt plans: "The schedule waits for no one, not even in the MOOC world." Echoing Sweeney's excuse of the "freeness" of the course, Warner (2013) proffered that "without sufficient incentive to catch up in my MOOC, one hiccup was enough to put me off track."

So, unlike Sweeney and Warner, I did finish—but just barely.

In June 2013, around twelve weeks after I had started "English Composition 1," I received an email that read in part: "Congratulations are in order for the 1289 students who earned a Statement of Accomplishment for English Composition I: Achieving Expertise. About half of those students had a score of 85% or higher. As such, I decided to award a Statement of Accomplishment with Distinction to those students." In other words, about 2 percent of the 60,000 or so participants who started the course actually finished it, though a significant percentage of those who did finish completed "distinctive" work. For what it's worth, my course score was 84.3 percent.

Comer and White (2016, 318) focus primarily on the validity of their assessment methods for "English Composition 1": they argue "that writing assessment can be effectively adapted to the MOOC environment" and that the peer assessment was similar to the expert assessment of a sample of portfolios from the course. Comer and White (2016, 346) only speak indirectly of the small percentage of students who actually finished the course in some fashion, though they acknowledge that it's difficult to conclude what this means in terms of the effectiveness of their MOOC: "Almost all students in English Composition 1 failed to achieve learning objectives; it is impossible to teach writing in a MOOC. Or, English Composition 1 was wildly successful, and we can teach writing meaningfully in a MOOC. Our data could offer evidence for either claim. Given the MOOC scale, it is highly unlikely that we could ever definitively conclude one way or another . . . The MOOC was likely better for some learners than whatever other educational alternatives were available to them; for many others, the MOOC was likely an inferior educational choice."

So, if the question is did "English Composition 1" work, the answer has to be "it depends." On one hand, based on the tiny percentage of participants who completed the course, the answer would have to be "no." On the other hand, because courses like this are usually taught in small sections, the fact that nearly 1,300 students *did* complete the course means the answer might also be "yes": "Comer teaches twelve first-year students a semester at Duke University in her academic writing seminar . . . it would take approximately fifty-three years for her to reach 1,289 learners" (Comer and White 2016, 346). So, even a small 2 percent completion rate represents a lot of students.

## RETURN OF THE MOOCS AND MY (BRIEF)
## ENCOUNTERS WITH "INTRO TO JAVASCRIPT" AND
## "COLLEGE ALGEBRA AND PROBLEM SOLVING"

The last MOOC I completed as a student was "English Composition 1" in June 2013, just a few months before the beginning of the end of MOOCs, when the excitement and anticipation of entrepreneurs and pundits (and fear and dread of most university faculty) of MOOCs disrupting the way universities function vanished like a bad dream. *Invasion of the MOOCs* was published in early 2014, and it already had the feel of a reflection on the recent past rather than a prediction of the coming future.

While I've mostly used my time since 2013 to be less a MOOC student and more a MOOC scholar, I did continue to drop into (and ultimately drop out of) a few more MOOCs. In summer 2014 I enrolled in the Coursera MOOC "Internet History, Technology, and Security," and I wrote about the experience as part of my essay "Always Alone and Together." The course was (and continues to be) taught by the University of Michigan's Charles Severance, who maintains a personal website and a social media presence as "Dr. Chuck." Severance has a PhD in computer science and a background in online education, having been the executive director of the Sakai Foundation in the early 2000s. "Internet History, Technology, and Security" was a survey course about the precursors and early days of the internet told through a series of video lectures, typical of most MOOCs. Severance also included archival footage of interviews he conducted in the 1990s and early 2000s with internet pioneers (it appears that Severance had aspirations to be a television host back then) and video of important sites in the history of computer science. This included a visit to Bletchley Park Museum in the United Kingdom, where Alan Turing and other members of the Enigma Research Section cracked the code the German Army used in World War II.

Severance's MOOC did quite a bit more than either Muller's or Comer's to reach out beyond the confines of the Coursera course shell with other social media platforms. Severance went another unique step further by holding "office hours" for his MOOC around the world. When I was enrolled in "Internet History, Technology, and Security," Severance held such get-togethers with MOOC students in Washington,

DC, Spain, Slovenia, Mexico, and Korea. He announced to the class the date and location of his office hours—typically at a public place like a coffee shop—and then posted to the MOOC brief videos (presumably shot with a cell phone) in which the students who showed up would introduce themselves. As he wrote in his essay "Learning about MOOCs by Talking to Students," "My goal for the face-to-face office hours was simply to better understand the various contexts where students were taking my courses. In a sense, I viewed them as ad hoc focus groups to help me improve my course" (Severance 2015, 174).

As I was preparing the draft of this chapter in fall 2017, I thought I should at least briefly relive my MOOC student days more directly. I registered for Udacity's "Intro to JavaScript," in part because I think it is an example of how MOOC providers have shifted away from higher education to the corporate sector and training, particularly those that are useful in the technology sector—like JavaScript. I registered for "College Algebra and Problem Solving" because it is one of the MOOCs offered in the edX platform from Arizona State University's Global Freshman Academy (GFA), the MOOC for college credit initiative announced with much fanfare in 2015. But I also registered for both of these MOOCs because I thought they were outside my comfort zone as a student. I was more comfortable at the outset with learning JavaScript, since I've been teaching basic HTML and CSS coding in advanced writing classes that involve website development and design for some time. I was *way* outside my abilities and comfort zone with the college algebra MOOC, as I'll get to in a moment.

For both MOOCs, there were some key differences in delivery compared to the MOOCs I had taken just a few years before. First, like most MOOCs since late 2017, both of these courses were self-paced and individualized, much more akin to the correspondence courses from early in the twentieth century. It wasn't until I enrolled that I realized that making the course self-paced meant it was no longer "Massive." Presumably, other people were enrolled in these courses at the same time I was, but without any interaction through peer review or discussion spaces, how could I tell? And what did it matter? I've already complained about the difficulty of conversing with MOOC classmates in the discussion forums and the wild inconsistency of the peer review process. I also noted the "loneliness" and isolation my grad students and I felt when we participated together in the crowded and active EDC MOOC. Yet the self-paced MOOCs with no other participants visible to me and no particular schedule or pace to follow somehow felt even less connected to others.

Second, it was more difficult in 2017 to find MOOCs that were truly "open." There were free courses available from Udacity, but they offered different levels of support or interaction, and there was no way to earn any sort of credential or certificate without paying a fee. The majority of Udacity's for-fee courses are available as part of a so-called nanodegree, which is available for a $199 a month subscription. Many edX courses were still free in 2017, but any sort of certification or credential was not, and if I wanted my "College Algebra and Problem Solving" GFA MOOC to count for college credit, I'd first have to pay a verification fee and then, after passing the course, pay for the credit itself.

I have yet to complete either of these new MOOCs, though for different reasons.

I'm likely to return to Udacity's "Intro to JavaScript" or a similar course hosted by one of the many competitors that offer online courses specifically about coding and the tech industry: Codecademy, Lynda.com, Treehouse Island, and Udemy, just to name a few. In late 2013 Udacity shifted its MOOCs away from higher education–style courses toward a focus on delivering instruction on workplace skills, sometimes about specific software packages. These MOOCs aren't necessarily for would-be college students or participants seeking an entertaining and self-fulfilling experience; rather, they are for people who are already employed or employable (albeit perhaps underemployed) who are acquiring or brushing up on new programming skills—like JavaScript, for example.

"Intro to JavaScript" offers detailed and straightforward instructions about what it promises, and those instructions include helpful videos, interactive activities, and quizzes. I didn't get far enough to understand how complete an introduction to JavaScript the course is, although given that Udacity estimates it should take most users over twelve hours to complete, my assumption is that it is thorough. And while I also assume that the course gets progressively more complex as it advances, I think I could (and perhaps will) complete "Intro to JavaScript" on my own.

But again, it lacks the elements that would truly make it a "course"; it certainly is not at all akin to a face-to-face course with other students, an instructor, assignments for credit, and so forth. Rather, it is essentially an interactive textbook, an online, multimedia version of those thick paperback books I used to pick up at bookstores with titles like *Teach Yourself HTML/CSS in a Week*, books I used to sometimes assign in classes I teach like "Writing for the Web." It is certainly the kind of content and delivery both Flexner and Noble would have described as vocational and not in the realm of what ought to be a subject of "higher learning." "Intro to JavaScript" was a fine learning opportunity, and perhaps it would have been a better experience had I paid the subscription fee, but it seemed quite different from the MOOCs I took earlier, which were trying to imitate a college course.

In contrast, my experience with the GFA's "College Algebra and Problem Solving" was almost a complete bust from the start. A lot of my unwillingness to complete this MOOC had nothing to do with the MOOC itself and everything to do with my own limitations and phobias with mathematics beyond simple addition, subtraction, multiplication, and division. I was an English major in college and went on to study writing and rhetoric at the graduate level because I enjoyed the subject area and was good at it. But at least part of my decision to stay close to English was to avoid math. The last math class I took, trigonometry, was in high school, and I still have no idea how I passed it, and for whatever reason (possibly because of other courses I had taken in high school), I didn't have to take the Gen Ed math course as an undergraduate. I registered for "College Algebra and Problem Solving" with the best of intentions of trying to face my math fears. But I couldn't overcome my own problems, and the self-paced and instructorless structure of the MOOC didn't help.

As mentioned, the GFA received enthusiastic press in 2015 when it was announced—this despite the failure of MOOCs reported by these same mainstream media outlets just a year or two earlier. The premise behind the ASU/edX partnership was that the MOOCs offered through the GFA could be used as actual college credit offered through ASU. First, students had to pay a $49 fee so ASU/edX could verify their identities. Second, students took the MOOC, and after they passed the course, they had the option of purchasing the ASU college credit for $200 a credit hour. It was an interesting innovation given that previous distance education courses collected the fee for the credits *before* the course began, not after the student completed and passed the course.

The heart of "College Algebra and Problem Solving" was a self-paced tutoring interface developed by McGraw-Hill called ALEKS (Assessment and LEarning in Knowledge Spaces). As noted in McGraw-Hill's press release about the GFA adopting this software for the course, "ALEKS provides personalized instruction, delivering the exact instruction students need, right when they need it. The ability to assist students at all levels using real-time feedback and inherent motivators results in significant improvements in retention, success and confidence" ("McGraw-Hill Education's ALEKS Adaptive Software Will Be Used in ASU's Global

Freshman Academy" 2016). Essentially, ALEKS is a modern and more robust version of the Computer-Assisted Instruction tools of the 1970s and 1980s.

For example, in a lesson on "using distribution and combining like terms to simplify" a univariate equation, ALEKS presented this equation with the instruction "simplify": $-4(w+6) + 6w$. There was a space to provide the answer, and there were also options to watch a video explaining the problem and how to solve it. There was also an "Explanation" button, which then showed the step-by-step process for solving the problem. Like Computer-Assisted Instruction programs of the past, ALEKS has infinite patience with slow learners like me: I could work through as many practice problems as I wanted for each concept. Once I was able to solve the practice problems successfully, ALEKS allowed me to move on to the next concept. It did "work" in that I was able to work through some of the early problems on my own with ALEKS (along with paper and pencil notes), but it took me quite a long time.

As far as I could tell from interactions with "College Algebra and Problem Solving," ALEKS was the only instruction in the course. There were videos and audio of unnamed instructors explaining the problems within ALEKS, but there were no other students or discussion forums and (at least for the free version of the course) no way to interact with some sort of live support or instruction. To complete the course, I would have first had to complete all of the assigned practice topics in ALEKS with 90 percent proficiency. I could then take a final exam (which appears to be the one and only assessment tool for the course), but only if I paid the $49 verification fee. After all that, if I passed the course with a C or better on the exam, I would be eligible to pay for the actual college credit for the course.

Now, I suppose if I absolutely had to earn a passing grade for a general education college algebra course, I could have worked through all of the exercises in "College Algebra and Problem Solving" and passed the test. But as blogger and community college dean Matt Reed (2015) pointed out in a critique of the GFA, trying to get ASU credit from the MOOC never made much sense because "that same student could take an actual course, online or onsite, from a community college" where the student would "have an actual instructor [to] provide actual guidance and feedback" and for far less than $200 a credit hour. Happily, I do not need general education algebra credits, and I gave up on this GFA course—and it would seem that I am far from the only one. According to McGraw-Hill's own press release promoting the benefits of ALEKS, the vast majority of "College Algebra and Problem Solving Students" give up. Between April 2016 and May 2017, the course "attracted 51,000 students across 196 countries," and the software was able to assess "more than 1,450,000 math skills for the 30,000 most active students" ("New Precalculus Course Is the Second Math Course Offered after College Algebra and Problem Solving Launched a Year Ago" 2017). However, only 613 students mastered all of the concepts presented by ALEKS, and it is not clear how many of those students paid for verification and took the exam.

These most recent MOOC experiences with "Intro to JavaScript" and "College Algebra and Problem Solving" suggest a mixed outlook. I thought "Intro to JavaScript" was the sort of topic and presentation that made sense, and Udacity as a provider seems to have found the right courses and market. According to Jillian D'Onfro (2015), Udacity was the first MOOC provider to reach profitability, in 2015. The reviews from past students/customers of its nanodegree programs are generally positive, though it is also clear that the results vary from student to student.

The future of the Global Freshman Academy is far bleaker, assuming its success and sustainability is tied to students paying for verification and transferable credit. In December 2015, Carl Straumsheim reported that less than 1 percent of students taking GFA courses were eligible to earn/pay for college credit. Straumsheim focused on a particular GFA course that drew over 34,000 "registrants" initially. Of the 1,100 who stayed active throughout the course, "323 now have the option of paying ASU an additional fee to receive credit," though it is unclear how many of even that less than 1 percent who were eligible followed through and sought the college credit (Straumsheim 2015). Based on email correspondence I had in December 2017 with representatives of the Global Freshman Academy, I do not believe the percentage of GFA students paying for verification and then credit has increased significantly since 2015.

As I will come to in chapter 4, dropout rates alone are not necessarily the best way of evaluating the effectiveness or value of a MOOC. It's a measure that doesn't account for the different values participants have for some aspects of the class (despite being unable to finish), and it certainly does not discount MOOCs generally as a learning opportunity. Nonetheless, the extremely low interest from participants in paying for transferable college credit from the GFA program is good evidence that this approach to MOOCs is not likely to replace institutional education anytime soon.

# 4

# MOOCS IN THE FACULTY CONTEXT

In chapter 3 I describe what it was like to be a MOOC student and also how MOOCs have changed. This chapter is about the context of MOOCs from the perspective of people who have taught and developed them—from inside the machine, so to speak. These MOOC faculty perspectives are vital. These voices bring expertise to the discussion about the present and future of distance education, MOOCs, and what comes next—as opposed to the pontifications and statements from pundits, entrepreneurs, and administrators that led to the sudden rise and fall of MOOCs in the first place.

## PROCESSES AND INTERVIEWEES

From the beginning of the process, I encouraged my interviewees to not be anonymous, and I was intent on including feedback from them in early drafts of this chapter. (Not all but many of the faculty I interviewed provided valuable feedback on this chapter when it was in process, and I am grateful to them for that work). I did this because I am persuaded by and indebted to the methodological approach followed by Cynthia L. Selfe and Gail E. Hawisher in their 2004 book, *Literate Lives in the Information Age.* Selfe and Hawisher trace the "digital literacy" histories of about twenty people who offer accounts about how it is they saw themselves becoming "literate," both in the traditional sense of reading and writing but also in the sense of becoming technically or computer literate. They could have taken the more conventional tack of presenting themselves as objective researchers making an argument based on their interviews and observations. But Selfe and Hawisher said this would have been disingenuous, and they wanted to resist the academic fiction of distance between the "observer and the observed" and to give their subjects the opportunity to both "talk back" and contribute to their account. "In other words," Selfe and Hawisher wrote in their introduction, "we asked how we could change our actual ways of working—of writing and interpreting—to learn

DOI: 10.7330/9781607327875.c004

more from the participants we studied rather than just about them . . . To our minds, co-authorship seemed a viable, practical, and ethical resolution" (Selfe and Hawisher 2004, 13). While I don't think "co-authorship" characterizes the ways my interviewees participated in the process here, it does seem more honest and authentic to offer them the opportunity to speak back and contribute to this chapter directly. Beyond that, it's important to acknowledge the partnership I have as a writer with the MOOC faculty I interviewed for this chapter because they do in very real ways act as both "subjects" of study and as expert sources.

To get the first group of interviews I conducted for this project in early and mid-2015, I reached out to contributors to *Invasion of the MOOCs* (Krause and Lowe 2014). They were:

- Denise Comer at the Conference for College Composition and Communication in Tampa, Florida. Comer is an associate professor of the practice of writing studies and the director of first-year writing in the Thompson Writing Program at Duke University. As I discuss in chapter 3, I was a student in Comer's MOOC "English Composition 1"; hers was the only MOOC I had taken offered by the people I interviewed.

- Karen Head is an associate professor in the School of Literature, Media, and Communication at Georgia Tech, and she is also the executive director of the Communication Center. She was a part of a team who developed and taught "Freshman Composition 2.0," the "GT MOOC." I interviewed her via Skype.

- The team behind the MOOC "Rhetorical Composing" at Ohio State University. This interview was conducted in a conference room on the OSU campus, and present were Kay Halasek (associate professor of English and the director of the University Institute for Teaching and Learning), Ben McCorkle (associate professor, OSU–Marion Campus), Scott DeWitt (associate professor), Susan Delagrange (associate professor and assistant dean of the OSU–Mansfield Campus), Cynthia Selfe (professor emeritus), and OSU graduate students Jennifer Michaels, Kaitlin Clinnin, Michael Blancato, and Chad Iwertz.

- Jeff Grabill and Julie Lindquist at Michigan State University were the lead faculty for their MOOC, "Thinking Like a Writer." Grabill is a professor of rhetoric and professional writing and also the associate provost for Teaching, Learning, and Technology; Lindquist is a professor in the Department of Writing, Rhetoric, and American Cultures at MSU. I interviewed them both in person at Michigan State (though, because of schedules, on different days) in spring 2015.

In fall 2015 I conducted two more interviews, this time with faculty not in composition and rhetoric. The first preferred to remain anonymous, so I will describe her here as Professor Jane Smith, a non-tenure-track faculty member at a large midwestern university teaching computer science. She developed and taught a series of MOOCs about web coding and development.

The second was with Gautam Kaul, the Fred M. Taylor Professor of Business Administration at the University of Michigan and also Special Counsel for Digital Education Initiatives in the UM Provost's Office. At the time of our interview, Kaul was discussing a MOOC on finance that he developed and taught through Coursera, though he has gone on to develop several other business administration and finance MOOCs with both Coursera and edX.

The interviews were transcribed (either by me or by a transcription service) and totaled just over 96,000 words. I reviewed the transcriptions and coded the text based on responses to specific questions and also themes that emerged from the conversations. What emerges from these interviews is a valuable look at the teaching context of MOOCs, what it is like to be inside that MOOC machine, especially in 2014–2015. Further, these interviews reflect on some of the assumptions we make about teaching—particularly the teaching of writing—in light of the MOOC "experiment."

### ORIGIN STORIES

For most of my interviewees, the origin of their MOOC teaching was closely tied to the opportunity of a grant from the Bill and Melinda Gates Foundation and happenstance. In November 2012—during the height of the so-called year of the MOOCs—the Gates Foundation announced that it had awarded a series of grants to teams at different colleges and universities to develop and experiment with MOOCs for introductory and general education courses. Among the funded MOOCs (which also included developmental and introductory MOOCs in math, the sciences, psychology, and political science) were introductory writing MOOCs offered by Ohio State University, Duke University, and the Georgia Institute of Technology. Halasek said, "I was talking with our associate provost for undergraduate studies on a different matter, and he mentioned to me that he'd seen the Gates Foundation call for MOOCs in general education, and he encouraged me to consider applying. And I really didn't feel like I could simply say no out of the gate." She solicited interest from her department at OSU, and McCorkle, Selfe, DeWitt, and Delagrange joined the team. Soon after that, the graduate students who were working on projects with these faculty members were recruited, again as a result of local circumstances and serendipity as much as anything else. For example, while trying to get paperwork signed by Selfe, Michaels "walked into this meeting that was marked on [Selfe's calendar] as . . . something like 'Awesome meeting with Kay' . . . And then I started hearing the conversation that, at one point, Cindy actually points at me and goes 'Jen would know something about that' because it was related to my research. And then I was on the train from there."

Comer's entry was similar, though the institutional context was equally important. Duke had already partnered with Coursera in developing MOOCs, and Comer had been approached by a professor who was teaching an engineering MOOC about designing a writing project: "I didn't know what a MOOC was. So he had to explain everything about it . . . and right away I began to see the complexity involved in designing writing for MOOCs. So I got interested in it." She, too, applied for and was awarded a Gates Foundation grant. The context at Georgia Tech was similar in that the school had also been an early partner with Coursera, though Karen Head was more reluctant to become involved: "I was volun-told . . . I really was drafted," primarily by her colleague and partner in developing the MOOC, Rebecca Burnett, to be the lead instructor of the course. "I was asked, sort of, originally to do it, and my initial response was no" because of a variety of other projects Head had underway and also because she worried about how a teaching commitment like this one would impact her case for tenure. In the prologue to her book *Disrupt This! MOOCs and the Promises of Technology*, Head (2017, 3–4, original emphasis) expands on this story and describes a dinner conversation she had with her husband about getting involved with the MOOC: "I assumed he would agree with me wholeheartedly. Instead, he asked me the question that would change my mind: 'Are you prepared to let others tell you whether teaching on a platform like this works—especially if they are already convinced it *will* work?'"

But important institutional missions and connections were also at play. After all, the MOOC faculty here all work at "R1" research institutions where experimentation is a part of the mission that also extends to research and scholarship on teaching. Grabill said, "I see Michigan State's [writing] program as one of the programs that has to do research . . . and that has to drive fast and take risks because we're protected in so many ways that our peers at other institutions are not, and we have the research capacity to do it." Comer said, "I'm interested in researching more about writing pedagogy in this context generally. Most of the questions that interest me are about how a particular context impacts writing pedagogy and what I can learn from it." The team at Ohio State expressed a similar motivation encouraged by the institution's research mission; also, as DeWitt pointed out, engaging in a MOOC teaching experiment as part of a research agenda was also a way of addressing the internal apprehensions of other faculty resistant to the idea and threat of MOOCs: "It becomes very difficult [for critics] to push back on somebody when you say, 'I'm getting into this because I want to investigate MOOCs and I want to collect some data and I want to do some research.' This is what we do in this department. It is our charge, our professional charge, in our department."

Institutional connections also lead to more interpersonal connections and motivations. Professor Smith was persuaded to get involved in developing and teaching MOOCs because of a colleague who had already had a great deal of success with Coursera and other online teaching initiatives. Kaul's involvement started with an email with the subject line "Do you want to teach thousands of students?": "Being in the business school I've gotten such emails before, and I was about to delete it. Then I saw the name of the person, and it sounded very familiar." This particular email was from a vice provost at the University of Michigan who was working out contract details with Coursera to be one of its early higher education partners. Kaul was also persuaded directly by Coursera's Daphne Koller: "She is a powerhouse, I mean both as an intellect and as a person, and she doesn't take no for an answer. So I not only agreed, I agreed to do it at the first launch of courses."

Of course, part of the motivation for these faculty to become involved in MOOCs was the hard to miss MOOC moment that was dominating headlines in the educational media at the time. Grabill said: "I became interested in the phenomenon . . . because it blew up in such interesting and quick ways . . . There was something kairotic about that moment." That moment corresponded with his interest in the "business of higher education" and the increasing importance of how we in higher education generally and in writing studies specifically demonstrate "value." He explains this further in his contribution to *Invasion of the MOOCs*: "The smartest people I have met in educational technology are focused on providing better education at lower costs. I take them seriously. For me, then, the current moment invites creativity and innovation, and while I am pretty sure that MOOCs as they are currently designed and implemented will not persist, I am confident we will see a number of innovations that will persist that have their origins in this moment" (Grabill 2014, 41).

Lindquist, Grabill's faculty partner for the MSU MOOC, had a different entry point into the MOOC. When Grabill asked her if she wanted to be a part of the MOOC, she said the idea "was entirely not on my radar. In fact . . . the very idea makes my stomach seize up for a couple of reasons. But that was the reason I decided to do it because that let me know that maybe I had some things to learn and I was too deep in my old commonplaces. I needed to have a disorienting experience."

Interestingly, none of the MOOC faculty I interviewed had a lot of previous experience teaching entirely online prior to developing a MOOC—though, as became clear during these interviews, the definition of "teaching online" was not entirely clear. Kaul had taught online in what he noted was a very different context: a global MBA program with a small group of students in Brazil whom he interacted with electronically and synchronously. This is not to say that the uses of technology in teaching and online culture were foreign to these faculty. For example, most had some prior experience with making use of online teaching tools in their otherwise conventional face-to-face classes. DeWitt said, "Before we ever used the term *hybrid*, I used to teach hybrid [classes] . . . using discussion forums. I did that in the [19]90s." When he was director of the first-year writing program at Ohio State, DeWitt oversaw an online space for peer review among many different sections of conventional face-to-face courses, a system that was eventually developed into an in-house peer review software product. But as Jen Michaels said: "I noticed there was almost silence when you asked . . . how many people have taught online. But [what if you had asked] how many of you have some sort of research or teaching experience in massive online communities?" In other words, while most of the faculty I interviewed did not have direct experience teaching online courses, they all had some experience with incorporating online teaching practices into their classes and some experience as researchers with online and social media spaces.

Head did have one experience with online education that distinguished her from her peers in these interviews: she had been a student in an online course. As part of her PhD studies and preparation for the language requirement, she took a conversational French course online. "I didn't like it," she said. "It got me what I needed from the standpoint of I wasn't doing it for the credit in the class, I was doing it to pass the exam. I had a very specific goal, and I didn't need to be able to speak French particularly well." Head took the class in the era of the first rise of traditional online courses I describe in chapter 1—"a good fifteen years ago, maybe," she said—and there were clear differences in the interactive technology available then. Still, "It just felt like there was an amorphous person out there."

It is also perhaps not surprising that most of the first wave of MOOC faculty had no experience in online-only teaching because of the nature of their teaching and research prior to becoming involved with MOOCs. The major MOOC providers—Coursera in particular—were interested in recruiting faculty from top-tier institutions, and fully online instruction was (and still is) unusual at these institutions. Head said: "I think we should have been talking to that group of people [who had been teaching online] from day one, and we didn't, and that was a huge mistake. But I think that, naively, a lot of people didn't think about talking to them." She went on: "Getting to know some of the people who've done distance learning for a really long time, like [Indiana University professor] Curtis Bonk, has been such an eye opener because . . . many of them were really angry about [how] . . . MOOCs became . . . kind of a metonymy for all things distance learning, which is of course complete BS."

At the same time, it's arguable that there are ways in which not knowing about the differences and affordances of teaching exclusively online was advantageous because it allowed these faculty to approach the experience without prior expectations. As Lindquist said, "I [had] the luxury of not being, not having any sort of historical identity as an online teacher or tech person particularly or an investment in making this my research field or in being known as the person who did this. Which gave me a lot of room to move."

## PRODUCTION VALUES: PLANNING AHEAD

With the exception of the writing MOOC at Michigan State, each MOOC described here was delivered through Coursera, largely because these institutions had prior relationships with Coursera. One of the results of this was the fact that MSU's MOOC was much smaller than the others (since there was no marketing of the course through Coursera), enrolling about 3,000 students the first time they offered it and about 2,000 the second time. Those numbers are still massive, but the other MOOCs taught by these instructors through Coursera had 20,000 to 80,000 students registered. However, I use the word *students* here cautiously since it's a problematic descriptive term, which I will return to later in this chapter.

Michigan State's and Ohio State's composition MOOCs also made extensive use of writing platforms that were not directly connected to the Canvas or Coursera platforms. Michigan State's MOOC made use of a peer review software called ELI Review, which traces its origins to

Michigan State's WIDE center. (WIDE formerly stood for Writing in Digital Environments and now stands for Writing, Information, and Digital Experience). ELI Review is now a for-profit tech start-up, and Grabill is one of the partners in the enterprise. The Ohio State University MOOC used a peer review platform called Commonplace—developed as part of DeWitt's earlier experiences and already in place at OSU—which was refined, recoded, and rebranded Writers Exchange, or "WEx." For Grabill at MSU, using the ELI Review software (which was in place and being used as part of MSU's writing program) was also part of the research and experimentation aspect of the MOOC, to see if the ELI software could be useful at such a large scale, certainly much larger than the typical use of the software in courses of twenty-five or so students. "It wasn't really the driver" of the MOOC, but, Grabill said, "it was a unique part of what we did."

The motivations for using WEx at OSU were similar in that they wanted to use a more robust peer review tool they didn't see available at the time with Coursera. DeWitt said:

> Something that I think that Coursera has done very well, they've created a peer review system that's trying to be as utilitarian as possible to meet the needs of the greatest number of people, doing the greatest amount of good, and [helping] all disciplines in every single course. They can't create a peer review system for every single discipline in an area . . . So I think that for what they created and for a lot of classes, it's been great, but it didn't do what we wanted to do, it wasn't created for a writing course. So we created WEx.

The MOOC environment and the Coursera platform presented some challenges in producing and changing materials that were clearly the result of the courses being online and of a "massive" scale. One of the most common examples of this that came up in our interviews was the problem of making changes and adjustments to the course. As DeWitt said, "I don't know anybody who actually teaches the syllabus day to day exactly the way they plan [to] because things come up . . . we're constantly adjusting." Comer agreed: "I have an entire syllabus developed before the class begins, [but] I don't have to have every single piece finished, I can have general goals, right? Learning objectives, learning outcomes, but I don't have to have every day, all five minutes of every single day of the semester planned out."

The inability to make adjustments might be as connected to the nature of teaching writing and related humanities-oriented courses as to anything else. Kaul described putting together the finance MOOC he taught as very straightforward (though he had taught it several times by the time of our interview). "Teaching finance is relatively easy," Kaul said. "I must admit if I were teaching [something more] unstructured . . . [A] colleague of mine . . . he's teaching [a] fantasy and science-fiction [MOOC] . . . To me, that's an achievement." But at least some of the challenge of planning and adjusting was related to the fact that the other instructors interviewed for this chapter had only developed and taught their MOOCs one or two times and often under unusual time constraints. Smith, who was simultaneously teaching and building a series of MOOCs on web development, noted the difficulty of addressing mistakes in her materials and how the reaction from students differed markedly in the online environment compared to the face-to-face classroom: "When I am speaking in [a face-to-face] class there's a general acceptance that, you know, you slip with the tongue and that's just a misunderstanding. But if you mess up on camera [or in other materials], you're incompetent. And again, with this high-pressure pace I'm doing, I don't have time to go back every time."

While the logistics of making changes to a course syllabus or correcting a mistake can often be complicated in a conventional online course, these problems were clearly worse as a result of having to deal with the intermediary of Coursera, the other tech support staff, and the sheer massive number of students. Head said Coursera "had a lot of really, really young people working with them, some of whom hadn't even gone to college. And it's like you're trying to explain things, your pedagogical reasons for wanting to do x, y, or z, and they think you're just being arbitrary."

Ultimately, the challenge seemed to also be about managing the many different pieces within each team's MOOC. As McCorkle said about the OSU writing MOOC, "We are laying out content several weeks ahead of when we are live. So . . . I remember vividly, week one, week two, managing discussion forums . . . Meanwhile, my brain also has to think about weeks four, five, and six, scripting stuff, making new arrangements . . . and thinking in those two parallel time lines is draining." Comer expressed a similar frustration. In working with a team of people—and, as I will describe in more detail later in this chapter, each of these MOOCs did require a sizable team of people both deeply involved in the MOOCs and behind the scenes—Comer pointed out that once the materials are completed, it's done: "So, if I get to week seven and I think 'darn, I should have really done this' . . . it's next to impossible to do it . . . Everything kind of funnels you in, and your options become much more limited as the course unfolds in development. And then by the time it's running, the learners had all kind[s] of great ideas for what I coulda/shoulda/woulda, and then they don't understand why I don't incorporate them."

Inevitably, the difficulties of making changes in the middle of the course meant that the course had to simply go on. Smith talked about how she learned there was no point in trying to correct every mistake— "you need to just let it go for a few sessions and then go back when everything is normalized."

## PRODUCTION VALUES: VIDEO "STARDOM"

Another production hurdle most of the MOOC faculty I interviewed experienced was the challenge of making the videos that served as the primary mode of delivery of information in the MOOCs. I say "most" because, once again, the Michigan State team took a different approach, without video instruction. Not surprisingly, recording video also presented teaching challenges because, like other components of the online course, videos have to be planned ahead and do not lend themselves to easy revision. For the MOOCs taught by Head, Comer, Kaul, and Smith, the MOOC videos were produced by staff at their institutions. Comer, Kaul, and Smith didn't raise any serious issues or concerns about this arrangement during our interviews, perhaps because of the presumed way these materials were handled by their universities and perhaps because they were pleased with the process and support. Comer singled out the support she received from the online course associate who worked with her on her MOOC because of her associate's experiences both in the field (she had a master's in English) and her expertise in course design and technology. "So when I was recording videos or designing modules," Comer said, her associate would remind her "'you forgot this, you have to add this,' or '[what] about this,' or 'I [don't think that will work out] the right way.' She gave me really strong feedback."

Head's experience was more fraught with challenges. The MOOC she was working with at Georgia Tech was one of three Gates Foundation grant MOOCs, and she said this additional work overwhelmed the video production staff: "We felt really constrained here because we had to work with the team that does videography in our distance education and they just weren't ready for this . . . The people at the day-to-day work level who were in the studios and stuff, they tried so hard, but they just didn't see this coming." Making changes/revisions to video is difficult enough, given the medium. Head said it was essentially impossible to make changes to her class videos without shooting another video, which, of course, meant returning again to the production staff charged with making the videos. Plus, the videos were expensive to produce; she said "almost all of the money that we got [from the Gates Foundation] went into videography, $34,000 of the $50,000."

The team at Ohio State was able to minimize these video production issues the second time it offered the MOOC by taking back control of the video process. DeWitt said that for the first version of the MOOC, the university did all of the production work, "and we were completely tied to their availabilities and workflow, and it was really, really difficult to work with." For the second version of the MOOC, DeWitt and his colleagues "took back" the video production. "It freed us up considerably to use some lower-tech options. We have a really great one-touch video recording room downstairs," which meant that when they were ready to record unit introductions and the like, "we could just step downstairs and record these. We could create a script, and I bought an app that was the teleprompter app for our iPad and we went down there, and we started creating all this stuff ourselves." DeWitt went on: "Our gut reaction was how great is it that we have all of these university resources, and it actually was far more difficult in some ways because we had to work with their workflow and we were completely held to their time schedule . . . I know iMovie and we can go down to the one-touch room, and we got this 99-cent app for a teleprompter and we suddenly were able to produce all those materials."

MSU's Grabill and Lindquist said they decided not to use video because they didn't see the role of lectures delivering "didactic information" in a writing course. In that sense the MSU MOOC seemed to have much in common with the first iteration of the University of Edinburgh's EDC MOOC I described in chapter 3: "It wasn't that we were worried about our tele-presence," Grabill said. "It was really a . . . pedagogical decision and an intellectual decision to see if we could scaffold something at [a large] scale that didn't rely on that kind of lecture content." All of the interactions Grabill, Lindquist, and their collaborators had with participants were through the assignments and "post-assignment sort of processing and reflection that we did as audio files"—in other words, debriefing after students completed assignments and with some podcast-like content. But as Lindquist said in her interview, it wasn't as if the idea of video content of some sort had not crossed their minds: "We had aspirations . . . We thought we would walk around campus, we would, you know, videotape us . . . learning different kinds of things, and we would include those kinds of pieces, too, a set [of] pieces to create an environment and a set of characters and all that." In addition to thinking that videos didn't fit with their pedagogical decisions, "it was too much, and on the time line we just couldn't" put together those video components.

While Kaul used video lectures extensively in his finance MOOC, he did raise questions about the importance of those videos in our interviews. "As I'm doing more advanced stuff, the videos are less and less important and the content and assessments are becoming big," particularly the assessments of the test questions and scenarios Kaul created. He added: "I believe we over-test our kids, but if you want to be learning on your own, if you are on your own, you have to figure out whether you're learning it or not. I would say that 90 percent of my time is on [developing] assessments and 10 percent on videos."

"Performing" for these videos also presented a challenge for most of the faculty I interviewed. Beyond some of the cultural and appearance issues I'll discuss later in this chapter, the basic recording of these mostly "talking head" videos—typically without an audience—was a disarming and uncomfortable experience, as most of the faculty I interviewed relayed. Recording video lectures certainly was different than the experience of face-to-face interaction with students in a traditional classroom, and it took some practice. Selfe said:

> It's different. We had takes. The first time we did this we had like five takes before I could actually get a word out. I had to do it with Scott [DeWitt]. In fact, that's one of the things I'd be forever grateful for. I couldn't do it. I couldn't make the words myself. And it wasn't until we could sit there and just pretend like we're having a conversation [that] I could get the thoughts out. So, you have to unlearn a lot of what you're concerned about, I think. And then once we left that behind we were better, I think.

With practice and with "taking back" the video production from their institutional video specialist, the teaching team members at OSU became much more comfortable and informal and conversational in their videos. Selfe said: "We became more and more informal and I think more relaxed and I think more human in our approach even to the materials. When we started the MOOC, we were very formal—you could even see it in our body language, [like] little blocks of wood, we would say 'Hello. My-name-is-Cynthia-Selfe,' and I'd look at a cheat sheet or something and go on."

The one faculty member who expressed no reservations about being on video was Kaul. "I love talking to the camera," Kaul said; he was as comfortable talking to me in our face-to-face interview as he was recording his videos with a camera and just one or two other people in the room. I'd suggest that part of Kaul's comfort had to do with his experiences as a performer in his younger days: "In school I'd been on stage a lot, so that didn't bother me."

## TEACHING ANXIETIES

For almost all of the people I interviewed, organizing and teaching a MOOC was a stressful and intense experience. The combination of the massiveness of the courses, the pressures of working on teaching materials far in advance and in collaboration with a team of both fellow teachers and institutional support staff, along with being publicly "out there" in teaching videos were all anxiety-inducing to different degrees and in different ways. All of the faculty and graduate students I interviewed were experienced classroom teachers, some having been in the role for decades. Yet some of the stories of nervousness and fears my interviewees told reminded me a bit of the stories some graduate assistants have told me about what it was like to teach their first sections of first-year writing.

While the MSU MOOC, at 2,000 to 3,000 participants, was small compared to the other Coursera-marketed MOOCs, the scale was still large and daunting. "Yeah, we [were] terrified," Lindquist said. Neither she, Grabill, nor anyone on their team had "any analogous experiences, so we just didn't know what would happen. We didn't know how big it would be, how explosive, how intense, how much interaction, how long a lot of people would stay around."

Karen Head had a similar feeling as the class began: "I was watching the numbers go up in the sign-up period and I was tracking them, and the bigger they got—and it was doubling weekly and I remember at one point just thinking, I don't want to do this. I don't want to turn this on, and I knew that I was past that. I had crossed that Rubicon." Dewitt pointed out that it wasn't merely the size but also the extreme "Open" part of the MOOC: "When I reflect and certainly when you [have] numbers like 21,000 or 30,000, that will kind of shake you a little bit. But I would say that when I think about [it,] a majority of our attention that went into the MOOC was about its massive openness, not necessarily its massive numbers. That's what made us rethink so much was the openness is at first 'oh, that was so massive.'"

Of course, while this massive group of students were mostly unknown to the MOOC faculty, the faculty who appeared on camera became disarmingly well-known to the students. As Head said, college faculty are "public figures" of a sort by virtue of teaching face-to-face classes, "but at least the admissions people have screened the students and we know who they are." That level of vetting of students does not take place with MOOCs, and it can be disconcerting. Head went on:

> I think suddenly being a rock star, it comes with its issues. You are going to have people who are going to make comments about you; you are going to have potentially stalkers; people want a piece of you in ways, and they think they are entitled to it. Our students feel that way about us now in our regular classes; they feel entitled to have our time and our feedback and lots of things, but you exponentialize that to 20[,000], 30[,000], 40,000 students all over the world, that becomes a very different thing, now suddenly you are doing a stadium show.

Head discussed the implications of the publicness of her MOOC presence for her own safety in some detail in the series of articles she wrote for the *Chronicle of Higher Education*. Her IT department at Georgia Tech "advised me to change my public e-mail address because there is a good chance that some students may try to reach me outside the course platform," which in turn might swamp her campus email, impacting her other Georgia Tech duties. "This conversation quickly led to a consideration of other potential privacy issues," including unwanted phone calls and even face-to-face visits from unknown MOOC students. At one point she was advised to temporarily move out of her office to a "more secure location." Head (2013) wrote that she "decided that all of this was ridiculous until some unknown person began repeatedly calling me."

Most faculty developed ways of coping with the scale and the openness. One way that manifested itself was finding strategies for being less in touch and involved in the class—essentially creating a distance from the teaching experience, especially after the course ran a second or third time. Comer spoke about how she didn't "even know exactly" when her MOOC began the second time because she wasn't as present "because [the first time] had been a fire hose for me . . . I had to back away from it; it was one of the most emotionally, um, vigorous experiences of my professional life." The course the first time around was "so incredibly taxing and demanding and time-consuming and gripping," and one way to deal with the scale of it all was by being less directly engaged.

Grabill's and Lindquist's approach to dealing with the massiveness was to essentially compartmentalize the different aspects of the course. For example, one of Grabill's tasks involved managing the peer review groups of participants so that students were fairly consistently put into groups of four active participants, a process that was time-consuming but manageable in parts. But as Grabill reflected in our interview, dividing up the work like this had consequences:

We were looking at our own little parts. That was the way we managed [the] workload, and there were also lots of things that we didn't do that we did in our other teaching lives. I don't think any of us found the experience of teaching a MOOC satisfying because it violated a set of, it violated all sorts of identity issues. Now, there's a downside to that because I think teachers, I think maybe writing teachers in particular . . . feel responsible for all sorts of things that they should probably just relax about. In terms of teacher engagement and teacher feedback and teacher response, I think we overdo it. Our colleagues in other areas don't overdo it.

The observation about "colleagues in other areas" is perhaps one of the reasons why Kaul did not seem to have the same level of anxiety about the MOOC experience as others, particularly the majority of my interviewees from writing studies. Kaul was surprised to find out on one of the first days of recording videos that 50,000 people had signed up for his MOOC—"that blew my mind"—but he still didn't seem that apprehensive about the process, certainly not of recording the video lectures: "Once I looked at the camera, whether there are 5 people there or 10,000, who cares. Only 1 percent is watching me at a time. It's not as if 1,000 people are sitting in a room together." Still, the massiveness of the course required him to make some compromises in how he approached the course. For his more traditional teaching, Kaul describes himself as "very close to students, so if you email me at 1:00 a.m., I'll respond to you, that's my attitude." This level of accessibility was obviously not possible with the MOOC. Kaul said he had to take a different approach with the MOOC by telling students "'don't e-mail me; we will have a set of tutors available to you, and if something becomes a problem, then I'll get it for you.' It was a very hard call I had to make because [the] first time I had 50,000 students. I'm not going to answer those e-mails."

The MOOC videos were also further complicated by faculty appearance and gender. My wife and I (she is also a college professor) frequently talk about the differences in how our students perceive and see us, and, unfortunately, students make a lot of sexist—even misogynistic—assumptions based largely on appearance and wardrobe. Essentially, my wife's and my general observations over the years have been that women have to dress up more than men to be taken seriously. This is particularly true in the lecture hall–size courses my wife occasionally teaches. It seems that students have similar (ill-formed) assumptions about MOOC instructors as well, and several of the women I interviewed said they were concerned enough to make choices about their appearance that went beyond the level of concern they have for this sort of thing in more conventional face-to-face courses.

In her essay in *Invasion of the MOOCs*, Comer (2014, 134) discusses the issues of online appearance (hair, makeup, and wardrobe) for herself and her colleagues: "While I should have been spending time doing something more intellectual, I've instead been rummaging through my wardrobe for different outfits, doing research on the best color patterns for the camera. I haven't been this concerned with my appearance as a teacher since the first weeks I stepped in front of a classroom."

Head's wardrobe concerns were as much about cultural sensitivity as anything else: "I made a very conscious cultural decision to look as modest as possible . . . I almost always had on sleeves, [though] interestingly enough, I chose not to cover my head and we had that discussion." Some of her clothing choices even became a topic of class discussion. Head said she wore "colorful things so they would pop" because so many of the people in the videos for other MOOCs she had seen were wearing "really dull clothes." Some MOOC participants wrote in a discussion forum "oh, I think she's trying to look ethnic and co-opt and appropriate other cultures," but then "a bunch of students came to my defense. This was all going on like a side conversation, and it was very funny . . . It's a very funny conversation to read through that had nothing to do with the class and everything to do with it."

In contrast, Professor Smith pushed back on these assumptions, mainly because of her approach to makeup and wardrobe in her day-to-day life: "I am a computer scientist by nature and that's [not] something that [I] . . . had to worry about as a computer scientist," she said. She noted how some people on Facebook would post about "how they won't leave the house without makeup, and I'm like, I never want my daughters to feel that way." This is not to say she did not initially feel a need to try to (in her words) "gussy up a little bit" because of the pressures of being on camera, and "who doesn't want to look nice?" So, Smith made a trip to a department store makeup counter and spoke with a consultant who "gave me a bunch of free samples, and [when they] ran out, I just stopped wearing it."

Smith's lack of concern or interest in prioritizing what she looked like to her students was also exemplified in this story she told me about the production process:

> When you do the videos, you never know what little screenshot they're gonna get . . . and the picture that the screenshot happens to take is me going [*at this point in our conversation, Smith purposefully demonstrated the ridiculous expression captured in her video thumbnail*], and everyone at work was talking about their glamour shots from that weekend, and I was like "oh, let me show you . . . the picture work put up for me." And they were

like "won't they take that down?" And I was like "you know what? I'm okay if they don't take it down because that's what I look like."

In the end, the complexities of how the faculty portrayed themselves (or found themselves being portrayed and perceived) seemed like an important aspect of the teaching experience, though it was one most of these interviewees had a hard time putting into words. In discussing the "compartmentalizing" strategy of negotiating the size of the MSU MOOC, Grabill also spoke of how that impacted his view of the MOOC as "disorienting" and "unsatisfying," as opposed to the scholarly approach to considering the MOOC phenomenon: "I didn't really like teaching the MOOC. I liked the MOOC, it was fun, it was an interesting phenomenon, but I did not like teaching it . . . Intellectually, I found it fascinating, I really enjoyed it. My embodied sort of affective emotional teacher response was often disorienting."

## DROPPING OUT VERSUS DROPPING IN

In the conversations I've had with MOOC faculty—both in this series of interviews and also with the faculty who contributed to *Invasion of the MOOCs*—I've never heard anyone with hands-on experience with teaching and designing MOOCs think of "students" in a MOOC as being like "students" in a traditional college class. Indeed, "student" isn't quite the right word for MOOC participants (even though it's the word I use since it's the one many of my interviewees used, and it is the most common term in most MOOC scholarship) because MOOC students come from a variety of places—in terms of geography and in terms of previous experiences and expectations—and they have various levels of commitment. It is probably best to think of MOOC students in more metaphorical terms. It's not unlike the use of the term *friend* in social media in the sense that, for most people, our Facebook "friends" likely include actual and real-life friends along with people we barely know or perhaps don't know at all.

Perhaps the most obvious way students are different and demonstrate a broad range of commitment to MOOCs is in the dropout rate. The vast majority of students who register for MOOCs do not complete them. For Comer's MOOC, the completion rate was about 2.5 percent, but, as she pointed out in our interview, "it depends on how I'm defining failure or success or completion. What I learned . . . is some faculty in MOOCs . . . might offer four projects, but if a student completes one of them, that's a completion. So, you can jimmy . . . what constitutes completion" and, presumably, what constitutes a "dropout."

Regardless of the specifics of what does and doesn't count as "completion," it's clear that the vast majority of people who actively engage in a MOOC (and the majority of those who sign up for a MOOC never engage in it at all) do not finish it, and this in and of itself offers a clear difference between students in a conventional classroom versus those in a MOOC—a difference that is relevant in the current era of higher education in the United States where institutions are under enormous pressure to improve retention and graduation rates. But again, the comparison between conventional students and MOOC students is misleading, and nowhere is this more evident than in the discussion of dropout rates. As Halasek said: "I sort of refuse to engage in an argument that talks about 'why are so many people dropping out from these courses' because that's enforcing, that's forcing our perceptions of what education is from within those bricks and mortar classrooms and from . . . pay-to-play models of education. When what I want to say is 'why are all of these people coming here? What is [it] that they desire and they think they can get from these spaces that encourages them to drop in?'" Selfe continued the point in our interview, adding that the term *dropouts* was "an artifact of the system that believes all students start at the same place, go through a sequence series, must go through every step, must complete every assignment . . . and that is not what was happening here."

Interestingly, the Ohio State team offered an "exit survey" from the course to try to find out more about why students left. Halasek said the overwhelming response was that students exited not because of the course per se but because of "personal life circumstances." The responses were typically "'I just don't have the time right now to devote what I've realized I need to devote to this course,' and it was a ten-week commitment." Grabill's experience with the MSU MOOC was similar: "Anecdotally, I had at least twenty-five people in each of the MOOCs who just reached out to me personally and said 'had a great experience, going on vacation' . . . So, non-completer, right? But really satisfied with the experience, 'got something out of it.'"

The small percentage of MOOC students who completed the courses also doesn't tell the full story of the relative success of a MOOC, since that small percentage is still an enormous number of students. Kaul said it depends on "your perspective, but even if you take—I think about 20 percent of them are bloody serious about it . . . that's a huge number" for a MOOC that has, for example, 50,000 registered users. And as Comer summed up in our interview (echoing a comment that would appear in the essay she co-wrote with Edward White [2016]), "I think 1,200 got statements of completion . . . the first time. So [the fact] that 1,200 people did that is, you know, it's either a miserable failure or incredibly impressive, I don't know."

## FROM EVERYWHERE BUT ANTARCTICA, AND WHAT WAS AND WASN'T EXPECTED

It wasn't entirely surprising that students in each of these MOOCs were as international as they were, though when I asked Grabill where the students in the comparably smaller MSU MOOC came from, he replied "every single continent on the damn planet with no marketing whatso-ever. Isn't that fascinating?" (Grabill also noted that there was a "little bit of marketing" through the Canvas course management system.) He went on: "That is not something to be overlooked; the world showed up . . . to our own little MOOC and we did not try very hard, right?. . . . I think there's tremendous thirst out there to what US higher education has to offer."

For Comer, reaching an international audience was part of her intent and why she had recruited Paul Kei Matsuda, the director of second lan-guage learning at Arizona State University, as a consultant. She said that in retrospect, the name of her MOOC, "English Composition 1," "sent the message to an international group of people that this was a course on how to compose in English. I don't think the enrollments would have been so high had I called it 'academic writing.'" And Head was proud of the international reach of the Georgia Tech writing MOOC: "We had students on every continent except Antarctica . . . I tried to actually get somebody from Antarctica at the station to sign up . . . [I] mean, we had a pin [on the course's Google Map] on Madagascar. And we had a pin in Greenland . . . We had pins in places where we knew students were actually risking their lives to view the content."

For the OSU team, the international composition of their MOOC was actually more of a surprise. Halasek said, "I was imagining a more US-based population, in part because I was seeing what we were doing through the lens of the Gates Foundation grant." That changed when they started reviewing the enrollment statistics provided by Coursera, a moment Selfe described as a "pivotal point": "Jen [Michaels] and I looked at those and we said 'This is not good. This is not what we had planned on doing'. . . . I mean, we started all of a sudden thinking about World Englishes and . . . our approaches to World Englishes." McCorkle said, "It became real to us at that point and we made those changes that Cindy [Selfe] described when we realized that there was a big chunk of people involved in this project that weren't just interested in learning writing so much as they were [in] learning to write in English. And that distinction, I think, bears underlining because that becomes a kind of a different mission than what we had originally anticipated."

"I think we were all rocked back on our heels a little bit by the experience," Selfe said. "It was like the hard disk was erased, it was, you have to see things differently and respond differently to that kind of environment." In other words, they needed to and did make changes to their approach for the course early on, adjusting the approach to a course where, for a higher percentage of the students, English was not their primary language.

The MOOC students were different from the students they encountered in their brick and mortar settings in other notable ways as well. For the OSU MOOC, Halasek relayed some of the basic demographics of the course: "Somewhere between 72 [percent] and 75 percent of the participants across the two MOOCs held bachelor's degrees or higher. The mean age, I think, was thirty-six, where . . . the mean age of undergraduates at Ohio State is, I think, twenty or twenty-one on the Columbus campus. It's slightly higher on the regional campuses. About 75 percent of the participants had English as a second, third, fourth, etc. language. About 75–80 percent of them were outside of North America."

DeWitt added that 68 percent of students said they were employed full- or part-time, and 31 percent were unemployed or didn't fall into a category where they considered themselves employed (a stay-at-home parent, for example). McCorkle recalled that about a third of students identified as belonging to an emerging economy. Comer's recollection of the demographics for her MOOC were similar: "There were slightly more women than men. But the majority of people . . . were age twenty-five to thirty-four, and they already had bachelor's degrees. Seventy-three percent were international, and most people actually said they were proficient in English already before taking the course" and were taking it for professional and career reasons. Of course, these students were self-assessing their English skills as "proficient," and it's probably fair to say that for most of Comer's students, English was not their primary language. Interestingly (and perhaps this fits with the stereotypes we have for these skills), about 70 percent of the students in Professor Smith's web development and coding MOOCs were men. She also said there was a strong European emphasis in the demographics. While Kaul and I didn't discuss the gender and demographics of his finance MOOCs in detail, he did indicate that about 70 percent of the students either had a college degree or were in college.

## THE ASPIRING CREATIVE WRITER AND THE
## LIMITED REACH OF "COMPOSITION"

One of the ways the MOOC student experience differed in the composition and rhetoric MOOCs versus Kaul's finance MOOC or Professor Smith's web development MOOCs had to do with the disconnect about the purposes of the MOOC. In addition to the differences in terms of "academic writing" versus learning to write better in English, many of the students who found their way into these composition and rhetoric MOOCs were, as Comer put it, a "cohort of learners [who] fashioned themselves as closet writers" and novelists. Lindquist said: "The way I describe [this] population of students we ended up getting is sort of the people with guitars in their basement who have no band or whatever. So they're writers who always wanted a community and didn't have access to one . . . I think they had sort of . . . unfulfilled identities as writers, aspirations. And they couldn't find an audience otherwise, and they didn't have access to any kind of writing community."

The OSU MOOC had a similar cohort of students who were aspiring writers seeking an audience. While the instructors tried to make it clear that their composition and rhetoric MOOC was focused on academic writing, they did suggest to these would-be novelists ways in which the MOOC could be useful to them. Halasek said, "Cindy [Selfe] came up with . . . a response to that: 'This is not a creative writing course. While we won't expressly be addressing those kinds of issues, the sorts of topics that we're engaging in this course will strengthen your writing.'" Selfe added that they did encourage "people who just wanted others to read their work to form groups outside of the class." Nonetheless, as Lindquist said about the MSU MOOC, this disconnect about the kind of writing taught and practiced was probably another part of the reason why some students "signed up early and checked out early."

In my interview with Grabill, he noted the ways this creative writing "mismatch" demonstrated the limited international applicability of a composition and rhetoric MOOC: "The composition course doesn't mean anything to anybody who's not in the United States," since the experience of "freshman composition" that is so common in American higher education is almost unheard of in the rest of the world. "So we had a lot of people three or four weeks into this [who] would say, 'By the way, what is a composition course?' And so . . . one of the things we learned is that a composition course MOOC that's going to engage the world is a bad idea." That's not to say, though, that there are no other opportunities to offer MOOCs about writing experiences that would have an international appeal: "They're very granular, but with the globe as your pool," there are plenty of opportunities for very focused writing courses. "So if they want [a MOOC] on songwriting, then we could do a MOOC on songwriting and everybody's going to know what that is. If you want a MOOC on writing a good sex scene in a romance novel, there are tens of thousands of people who would sign up for that."

Professor Smith expressed a similar mismatch, not so much based on misunderstanding the subject of the course but on the ways students find others to work with within a MOOC: "We need to combine MOOCs with OkCupid," the popular dating application. "You know, group [students] based on somewhat self-selecting but not completely self-selecting, based on 'oh hey, you want to take this course? We have a group, we got a study group for you.'"

## STUDENTS' EXPECTATIONS AND COMPLAINTS; STUDENTS' GENEROSITY AND INDIVIDUAL SUCCESSES

Many interviewees mentioned moments in their courses when students expressed frustration and dissatisfaction with their MOOC experiences. Sometimes, these were small details; for example, one of the things Kaul said in passing about putting together the videos for his class was "you wouldn't believe how irritated people get if they click on the video and it doesn't work" right away. Lindquist noted that sometimes students would express their frustrations about the course being "too hard" or "too easy," which is probably inevitable for any massive and open course where there are no prerequisites or separation into class grades that define the hierarchy in more conventional education. "The interesting thing is that it was free, so it wasn't as if people had made a bad investment," Lindquist said. "And yet, they really felt . . . betrayed somehow. That's an interesting theme to consider, what kind of, you know, emotional or whatever investment they made and how that was betrayed in some kind of way . . . It was only a handful of students considering the mass that we had, but those were the things we couldn't have predicted and spent a lot of time trying to troubleshoot and problem-solve because they were real presences in this community."

The problems of "trolling" between students in discussion and peer review groups—while not absent—were fairly minimal, which is perhaps surprising considering the regular opportunities for miscommunication in those groups. Generally, students directed bad behavior not at fellow students but at MOOC faculty. As previously noted, there were the concerns Head had about being stalked by MOOC students. Professor Smith said, "The trolling seems to be directed at me and not the other students." Some of these students tracked down her email address to contact her directly with what she described as "mean emails." Smith said her colleagues and administrators at her university were "getting a little upset" about what she (and other MOOC instructors) were experiencing from angry students, and there was talk with Coursera about policies to essentially kick students out of MOOCs for harassment.

Comer (along with Ryan Baker and Yuan Wang) published an article that explores this in more detailed and subtle ways (2015). Using their MOOCs as case studies (which were Comer's "English Composition 1" MOOC and a MOOC taught by Baker and Wang called "Big Data in Education"), Comer, Baker, and Wang note the many ways negativity about many different aspects of the courses emerged, and they argue that it certainly contributed to learner disengagement and instructor burnout. They also suggest ways of anticipating and limiting such negativity from future MOOC and online teaching experiences (Comer, Baker, and Wang 2015).

But mostly, MOOC faculty were impressed with the extent to which the students who were engaged in the course worked together. In fact, one of the more interesting aspects of these interviews was how, even in these very large online courses composed of anonymous and far-flung students, most of the faculty I talked with had specific stories of student engagement and individual student success. While lamenting the trolling from some students, Professor Smith also said she was "shocked" by how supportive of each other many of her students were: "these people get on [the class site] and they're just there to help people." Head described the ways she and her colleagues were able to better connect with students outside of the Coursera platform and how that led to a community of Russian students "who actually translated our entire site. Everything. Now, we fortunately had a postdoc fellow who was Russian" who was able to double-check what the students were up to. "My running joke," Head said, "was we were . . . running . . . a backdoor way for the Russian mob" and "they were running drug money." Of course, the translations checked out as legitimate: "The sense of . . . community and spirit and esprit de corp, the way that students helped one another and talked to one another, you know, I'm still trying to take lessons from that and figure out ways to integrate that into smaller classes."

Kaul relayed a similar "collaborative" experience, though on a somewhat smaller scale. He said he discovered a group of five students in one office in another country who were taking his finance MOOC. "So . . . one person would email me regularly. I said 'you shouldn't be doing that,'" in part because of Kaul's previously mentioned policy of not responding to individual student emails. "But I felt compelled to respond, and during lunch break I was on the screens of everybody. So, they decided to go to Starbucks in town and do homework together."

And despite the thousands and thousands of student participants in these MOOCs, several of the faculty I interviewed had detailed and inspiring stories about the experiences of individual students. Lindquist told a story about getting phone calls from students who were "so inexperienced and alienated from the technology" that they needed basic help with the course. She told me this story about such a student with whom she spoke on the phone:

> So, one woman in particular who said, "How do I get on this [MOOC]?" And I said, "Well, you know, you go to your computer." She says, "I don't have a computer yet." "So, well, you're going to need one of those." I had another conversation with her after she went out and bought a computer for this purpose and . . . the stakes are high because . . . a working-class woman in a remote area and a rural area, you know, this is what she's trying to do. I was trying to get her to log on . . . "What's an ID?" she wants to know, and I tell her, "you know, usually it's just your name," and I said you need to put in a password. She said, "What's a password?" And she said, "Can it be my ID?" and I said, "well, no, the ID is to make it sort of mysterious so that people can't figure it out," and she said "well, if I just make it up, won't the computer know that I'm just making it up?"

Ultimately, Lindquist's student stayed "around for a while" but not for the whole class.

The OSU faculty had some similarly interesting stories of individual student successes. Halasek recalled a student who had taken the MOOC to improve her English skills and who also revealed that she cared for her elderly parents. At one point, she wrote about how "she was finding herself winning more battles than losing them" in her day-to-day life of communicating with medical and care professionals about her parents. Halasek said, "And so that's another way that she leveraged the learning . . . And so in that case it was, I would say, writing in English, I would say also it was rhetorical . . . proficiencies in English for her personal purposes or professional purposes." Selfe recalled a similar story of self-empowerment: "There was the eighty-three-year-old grandmother that published her first piece of writing . . . She published her first piece of writing, she got it published after she had taken the MOOC and she was something like eighty-three."

These anecdotes about individual students are a powerful reminder of the difficulty of measuring "success" of students in MOOCs and also of how it's really not possible to use the same tools of assessment we use in conventional higher education settings—retention rates, grades, dropout rates, and so forth. As Halasek said in talking about dropout rates during our interview, those statistics and these kinds of individual stories exemplify the difficulty with defining "learning" or "success" for MOOC students:

> I've talked . . . about how we need to redefine what we mean by student success in MOOCs because it's not driven by faculty assessment of student writing in our case because we did no faculty assessment of student writing. So, if we don't have a typical bricks and mortar understanding of assessment, yet we know folks are succeeding [because] they're getting things published or they're succeeding in having arguments with medical professionals and seeing a result of their now newly found . . . skills or newly developed skills. So, I always think we are asking all of the wrong questions when we [talk about success], although it is the critical question, but this is always being answered. I give . . . responses like "why are we talking about dropout or . . . ?" because to me it's more like drop in, right there.

## TEACHING IN THE MOOC VERSUS FACE TO FACE

Comparing MOOCs (and online courses generally) to conventional face-to-face courses—particularly in terms of which is "better"—is not the point. It's similar to comparing speaking with someone in person versus on the phone versus texting with them: there are similarities among all three, but they all have different purposes, advantages, drawbacks, and affordances. What's more important is what's possible in these different situations. That said, it was difficult for these faculty to not compare the experience of teaching in a MOOC versus teaching a traditional face-to-face course.

As the previous sections discussed, the MOOC students were quite different from the students these faculty work with in their face-to-face university courses. Similarly, the expectations faculty had for MOOC students were different than those they had for the students in their traditional courses. Professor Smith commented on this difference between her MOOC students and her traditional students. While her more traditional students might be overly focused on grades at the expense of learning, Smith said "they work very hard for those grades, and I find with the MOOCs, they don't . . . realize that you need to go beyond what is being required here; they don't see the other people around them studying or trying things." Comer had a similar observation about presenting her class to the right level. She wanted it to at least approach the level of rigor she expected from her students at Duke: "And yet [at] the same time [the Coursera developers] are telling me 'well, these are people who are doing coursework while they are doing dishes, and, you know, after they've worked a long day and they're coming home and doing it.' I mean, I really admire people who are trying to build more into their lives like that."

Ultimately, I think it's fair to say that most of the faculty I interviewed for this project—even the ones who were and remain enthusiastic about MOOCs—still believe the kind of face-to-face instruction they are doing in their universities is superior to what they are offering in their MOOCs, and this state of affairs is likely to continue. As Kaul put it several times in our interview, "I believe face-to-face interaction is the ultimate key" in education, and MOOCs "can only go so far." MOOCs are not a replacement for face-to-face education but a starting point that can lead to a more traditional education.

Head said that even some students who one would think would be particularly interested in the online-only format had reservations. She told a story of teaching a technical communication course to a group of computer science majors: "If ever there was an audience that I thought would be keen on [the MOOC and online formats], it would've been them." She recalls talking to this group of students during the planning phase of the MOOC she would be teaching and asking what they thought about the all-online format. Head paraphrased the conversation: "They were all like 'look, we love the fact that we can go out and get additional information, but we see this kind of thing as like another textbook or study guide or another way to hear something, but we absolutely do not want to get our education this way.' And I said, 'Yeah, but you're always complaining about how 'I don't want to come to class," and they were like, 'yeah, we do that, but we still actually really want to come to class.'"

The one exception to this view came from Grabill, who said in passing in our conversation that one of the topics that resurfaced in the initial spike in MOOCs "is to try to re-inscribe something that I thought was dead and buried, and that is that face-to-face education is better than online education. There's no evidence that that's true." As I have suggested throughout this book, I agree with Grabill's position, though Grabill was speaking about online education in its more conventional forms rather than the experiment of MOOCs.

That said, the MOOC teaching experience has impacted at least some of my interviewees' more conventional classroom practices, which was one of the reasons why some of these faculty decided to create and teach a MOOC in the first place. "That was something that the associate provost who funded us the first year wanted, the feedback loop, wanted our own campus program to learn and change," Grabill

said. "We didn't transform our own campus first-year writing experience because of it, but we did learn from it, we did learn some adapta-
tions," including what he described as a "studio model" of instruction
for first-year writing where two or three instructors combine classes
for some larger group moments, followed by breaking students into
smaller groups.

Some faculty reflected in personal, albeit abstract, terms on the
differences between the MOOC teaching experience and their more
conventional teaching experiences and the ways the MOOC made
more visible to them some of the things they rely on to be an effective
classroom teacher. For example, speaking about the discussion forums,
Comer said her teacher instinct for normal classroom dynamics is to
get involved: "If there's trouble, let me understand if it's trouble to be
addressed or that can be let . . . lie or just grumbling or what is it." But
in the large MOOC discussion forums, "I had no frame of reference for
handling trouble." The team at OSU was more involved regularly with
the discussion forums—in part because they were a "team" and it was
more possible to divide up that labor—and that represented a different
teaching dynamic. Halasek said, "I think about how do I contribute to
and facilitate the discussion" in a conventional class, "but I don't think
in terms of where do I step in to same degree that we did in the MOOC,"
where the instructor intervention was much more intentional and less
instinctual than it is in a smaller face-to-face course. Lindquist said the
MOOC experience made more visible to her the extent to which she
knows "certain performative moves" to make based on her experiences
and the immediate reactions of students in the room:

> I feel like I can frame this, I can handle this, I can manage this, I can
> charm this person, I can tell a joke, there are all kinds of things that I can
> do that are unrelated to the curricular design. I have great faith in my
> ability to sort of be a certain kind of person to make things happen—to a
> fault . . . And it was interesting to have an environment in which I couldn't,
> I didn't have access to any of those things . . . I was completely abstracted
> as the person I am in the classroom from that moment, so students, I just
> wasn't encountering student in fragments, they were encountering me
> and all of us as fragments as well.

Others noted practical lessons learned from the MOOC experience
that they have brought into their conventional face-to-face classrooms.
Professor Smith spoke about the challenges of teaching web coding
because "for what I am teaching, it can't be a TED talk, it can't be . . .
broken up into ten to fifteen short, entertaining videos. I need to cover
boring, basic stuff so you can type it in and hopefully once you got

those basics, you can start having fun." Still, she said, "Coursera has improved my thought process," and she has worked in both her MOOC and face-to-face classes at breaking down her teaching into "smaller chunks" of instruction. Kaul spoke similarly of the "very intense experience" of creating course content he delivered in his courses "physically in a classroom to online. I'm being challenged, but I have learned and grown tremendously." He's taken what he's learned from the MOOC teaching experience to change his approach to his face-to-face courses, too. Kaul said, "I'm . . . using that same content to flip stuff . . . Now I don't teach content anymore, I just show up and do problems" with his students. "My classes changed [and] at least 50 percent of the content is gone out of the class where they're expected to know it . . . They have all the resources I provide them . . . Their opportunity to learn outside the classroom has jumped dramatically."

## THE "STUDENT-CENTERED" VERSUS "TEACHER-CENTERED" COURSE

One question I asked each of my interviewees was about their perceptions of the extent to which the MOOC proved to be a "student-centered" versus a "teacher-centered" experience. I was interested in their response because in my experiences as a MOOC student, I thought the format was very much teacher-centered.

When I asked Comer this question (recall that she was the first person I interviewed for this project), I must say I was taken aback a bit by her response to the question, which I awkwardly phrased as more of a statement—"there's something about MOOCs as very teacher-centered as opposed to student-centered in the way we talk about this in composition." "I have the total opposite impression," Comer said. She went on, adamant on this position:

> It is true that I designed the writing projects and I did the videos and I constructed the [course], but the actual unfolding—the actual course as it is experienced by the learners—seems to me that they make it what they want of it completely, COMPLETELY . . . To the 'nth degree in comparison to student-centered learning that happens in my seminar space . . . In the MOOC, they can do it and then be rewarded for it and feel like it's okay. And I think that's all right, actually, because they come . . . I'll set out learning objectives in the MOOC, and you might go and have your own learning objectives, and . . . then maybe you go away and that's nothing to do with my learning objectives.

Selfe expressed a similarly strong take on the student-centered nature of the MOOC:

I think it would be a mistake to think that the teacher is the center of this MOOC. For me, that is so not what happened . . . It's all the activity that was at the center of this course, the student interaction and the ways in which students helped to teach each other, not to say that there were no course materials with the second [version of the course] that we made, we did. So we provided a stage within which that interaction happened and instruction, but it was the interaction and the students, shaping of that stage that was massively open to many.

Grabill felt just as strongly about MOOCs as a teacher-centered space, saying "I have learned to distrust many of my own perceptions on what's going on in the learning environments I'm responsible for." He continued: "I think no teacher that you talk to, and I'm included in this, ever wants to say 'oh yeah, I designed this teacher-centric thing and it rocks. It's all about me.' Nobody wants to admit to that, although I will tell you that the next generation of MOOC enthusiasts on this campus are in it because they really want to be that guy on the stage." Professor Smith expressed a similar sentiment about her web development MOOCs:

It's completely a sage on the stage . . . the deliverables that I am providing are very much sage on the stage . . . It's not easy to create student-centered experiences to go along with the lectures because they're not together, they're not peers. They can self-select peers and we can provide them [with] resources to help them find where they should go . . . So, [for an instructor to take] a student-centered approach, I think it's a deadly idea because . . . how can I relate to every student from a student-centered perspective? You'd freeze. So, at some point, [I've] got to pick my denominator, this is the denominator I'm got to teach to, I'm [lecturing] to, this is it right here.

But perhaps not surprisingly, most of the responses to this question from faculty were more complicated and mixed. McCorkle pointed out that the basic design of Coursera and similar MOOC delivery platforms enables a teacher-centered approach: "It is very easy to shoot talking head lecture videos, put them out there, pin quizzes, use discussion forums in such a way that you're talking about ways of supplementing the thing that you learned in this main area, voila." But students can and do push back to upset this structure: "It's like nature finds a way, it's like *Jurassic Park*." McCorkle said students "hijack discussion forum threads, and I mean that in the best possible way. They go outside Coursera and set up Facebook groups and Google Plus groups. They basically push past the boundaries of [the course] in ways that resist that infrastructure in a healthy way."

Two of the graduate students working on the OSU team, Iwertz and Blancato, shared an excellent example of students hijacking a discussion forum in healthy ways in a discussion thread titled "Are the instructors going to teach us anything?" The thread, which generated a tremendous number of responses, eventually came to be an exchange between one student and DeWitt. Blancato said it was difficult at times to figure out who were the instructors and who were the students:

> There were many moments [in the discussion thread] when a student comes in and says, "I want to be taught rhetorical concepts and I do not feel like I'm getting that out of the course right now." And then a student will jump in and point out all the ways in which the student is using rhetoric to persuade others. And that happens throughout that thread, throughout the discussion boards, and even Scott [DeWitt] said in that "Are the instructors going to teach us anything?" thread that he's learned a lot. So the teachers are learning from the students. The students are learning from other students. It's really hard to pinpoint exactly who the instructor is.

In other words, even for the participants in the MOOC as it was happening, the "centeredness" of students or instructors—even the role of who is acting as a student or as an instructor—was contested, debatable, and a matter of individual perceptions.

The teacher-centered/student-centered perspective also depended on what aspect of the MOOC experience students and teachers were examining. "It's entirely teacher-centered if you're talking about the videos because it's all about you," Head said. "I think it's true that it's not as teacher-centered when you're talking about the discussion groups, when you are talking about the ways students help one another." She also noted that the "team-teaching" aspect of the OSU MOOC, where several different faculty appeared in the videos, probably helped make the teaching more "de-centered" than MOOCs (like Head's MOOC from Georgia Tech) with a single professor "starring" in the course videos. Kaul echoed this question of perceptions. He acknowledged that most MOOCs are centered around faculty videos to a "casual observer." "But to a real learner, no. My videos actually become totally irrelevant to the serious learner," Kaul said, because the real learning takes place where students work through the problems of the course, which is why Kaul says he spends more time now designing the problem sets and assessment for those problems than on anything else in the MOOC.

The challenge remains, though, how to design MOOCs effectively with elements to draw students in and that make faculty visible—like videos—while pushing students to actively engage in activities that allow them to make connections to other students and in which they complete tasks (participating in discussions, writing and reviewing essays, solving the problems of a finance class, completing the coding for a web development class, and so forth) that can be assessed in a meaningful way. "Design matters tremendously," Grabill said. "Yes, really good students can make really good experiences out of it," meaning more teacher-centered xMOOCs; they "can do things that are contrary to design. There's no question about it. It doesn't mean that that's the experience that most students had."

## THE FUTURE AND THE NOW

By the time I conducted these interviews in 2015, the exuberance about MOOCs had settled into a steady backlash about their failure and dim future in higher education. I think this is important to mention because it helps define the context in which I asked the faculty I interviewed to speculate on the future of MOOCs.

I'll close this chapter with some of my interviewees' thoughts on the future. But before getting to some of the possible implications of MOOCs in the coming years, in terms of both lessons learned and how the technology might change higher education, it's important to note some of the issues of the longer-term sustainability of MOOCs.

For the most part, the tenure-track faculty I interviewed for this chapter developed and taught their MOOCs with no direct financial compensation. Kaul indicated that there was a "very small stipend" initially, though he said he was motivated "mainly to learn for [myself] and hopefully to add value to the institution." Professor Smith and I didn't discuss compensation in any great detail, but I think it's fair to say that she was being paid from Coursera for her courses, and Comer (who is still teaching her MOOC) suggested that there was some "profit sharing" with her MOOC. But in both cases, I think this compensation was modest. At the same time, it's probably not fair to characterize this work as entirely "for free," since most of the faculty I spoke with were compensated with released time from other teaching, other duties on campus, and so forth.

It became clear in these interviews that all of the MOOCs—even the ones funded in part by the Gates Foundation, even the comparably small MSU MOOC—relied in significant ways on the financial support from their universities, and these MOOCs were all offered through large research universities with deep pockets. The team from OSU spoke about internal grants from their university, graduate assistant support, and a variety of technical resources. Head pointed out that even as policymakers and media pundits might be "looking for easy answers" and considering MOOCs, the reality is that it's a cost-prohibitive model, especially for courses like writing that depend on qualitative decisions from readers to make evaluations. Both Head and Comer said they had about twenty people involved in their MOOCs in different ways, staff people who all needed to be paid. The MSU MOOC was quite a bit smaller, just Grabill and Lindquist along with three other teachers and a graduate student. Grabill said there was "value" in the sense of MOOC research as an intellectual activity, as a way to enhance institutional reputation, and as a marketing tool; he also argued that the costs went down in the second year they ran their MOOC, since they had already developed materials. But as Grabill said in discussing the success of creating an environment where students could "learn writing at scale," he discovered it was possible, "but it's really hard and it's not cheap."

In short, the sometimes stated (and usually implied) hopes university administrators and education entrepreneurs had of replacing college courses—particularly courses taught in small sections, like first-year composition and rhetoric—with MOOCs have faded for many reasons, including costs and sustainability. MOOC providers and universities cannot rely on the free labor of educators indefinitely. As McCorkle said, "I have no head for business or anything like that, but I think people are going to be sorely disappointed" if they think MOOCs will be financially sustainable if "we can just charge people $250 to take a MOOC course" and they believe in the viability of that course actually converting into transferable college credit. And as several of the MOOC faculty I interviewed noted, charging students for credits or participation means the MOOC is no longer "open." If a MOOC is no longer open, Halasek said, "then you have something else. Then you have something that is not a MOOC."

Still, in light of their experiments with MOOCs, I pressed the faculty I interviewed to imagine what the future of higher education might look like within the context of MOOCs and other predictions. Some did this reluctantly. Selfe was humorously shocked at the question, responding initially, "how can you possibly think that we could respond," which brought laughter to the room. But then she did respond:

> The pace of change has become so rapid, especially in digital environments and teaching environments, and the converging forces of globalism and economic pressures and regionalisms are so varied, I don't think I could respond to [your question]. But I do know this: it will not be the same as what we're facing right now, and I don't think MOOCs are going to be an issue. I don't think the bricks and mortar classroom we have right here is really going to be an issue. They're going to be very

different animals, very different contexts for education. And it's going to be changing rapidly in response to all sorts of factors that we're starting to feel right now.

Comer suggested something similar. MOOCs and their aftermaths might "shake up the idea that the ideal path to a degree . . . needs to be consecutive and linear and all within the same institutional walls." While there are ways now for students to build a degree with credits from different institutions and over a period of time, Comer was imagining a situation where it would be more systematic and common for students to put together a degree with courses "taught by people from the University of Edinburgh at the same time as [professors from] Duke or Ohio State." Kaul thought there might be a similar alternative to the traditional degree from something like the certificate programs currently offered by MOOC providers: "Universities have had a monopoly of granting certification, and I think the good thing is that we are now trying to think about what that certification means because another avenue of certification has opened up." At the same time, Kaul believes strongly in the value of face-to-face education as we know it, and he doesn't see its value waning with the rise of online programs or certificate options: "Do I think that face-to-face education is going to disappear? No. I think it will become more important. Because you can now figure out what the value of it is."

There is also the future of MOOCs beyond higher education as we know it. Grabill and others I interviewed noted how the for-profit MOOC providers have shifted their emphasis away from universities and higher education and toward training and professional certification programs. Within universities, MOOCs might also have a role not as courses per se but as textbooks or, as I discussed with Lindquist, as "professional development" experiences. She went on to imagine people "learning to teach in the secondary schools," perhaps current or future teachers who don't "have access to a larger network of people" also learning about teaching in secondary schools for one reason or another. MOOCs might serve as a means to reach those students.

As was the case with correspondence study, radio and television courses, and traditional online courses, no single technology is likely to be the overwhelming driving force to "end," let alone change, the university as we know it. As Michaels said, if it were as simple as simply "selling" courses and credits, "correspondence courses would've killed the university 100 years ago." The system is too complex; "it's like the rain forest, you know," Kaul said. "You just can't take out one tree and say that the rainforest will disappear."

# 5

# THE PRESENT AND (FUZZY AND DIFFICULT TO PREDICT) FUTURE OF MOOCS AND BEYOND

In chapter 1 I describe the rapid rise and fall of MOOCs as a disruptive force in higher education. They certainly did not live up to the dreams of their founders and the hype in the media. I explain three of the key reasons why MOOCs have failed to change universities: the problem of "scaling" to provide institutional education (particularly as it relates to assessment), the underestimation of the historical depth and breadth of higher education, and the fundamental misunderstanding of who would want a MOOC credential and why. I argue that these failures are also in part a result of MOOC entrepreneurs not understanding the history of distance education innovations, the needs and motivations of most students, and the challenges faced by MOOC instructors.

However, as I also noted in chapter 1, it would be a mistake for distance education skeptics to assume with a mix of relief and happiness that the MOOC moment is over and there is no reason to pay attention to them anymore. MOOCs continue to succeed (albeit in more modest ways than the founders of Udacity and Coursera would have preferred), and their futures continue to influence experiments with distance education. Further, the delicate partnerships between nonprofit educational institutions and for-profit educational companies is becoming more complex and fluid. Most American universities and colleges have given up on MOOCs as part of a rational way to deliver institutional education. At the same time, most American universities and colleges are working to develop more online programs and degrees, arguably encouraged by the MOOC moment, and most nonprofit institutions are pursuing these programs with for-profit Online Program Management partners.

This closing chapter is about this present and difficult to predict future. Picking up where I left off in chapter 1, I begin by describing the ways MOOCs have and continue to succeed, particularly as a means of delivering training and learning opportunities outside

DOI: 10.7330/9781607327875.c005

of institutional education. Then I offer two predictions and a warning of what could be in store in the near future of higher education in America, particularly in relation to the increasing role of Online Program Management companies.

## HOW AND WHY MOOCS SUCCEEDED IN
## HIGHER EDUCATION AND BEYOND

Relative to their failures, especially their impact on the way higher education works in the United States, MOOC successes have been modest. It's also hard to describe MOOC success because while most of the failure of MOOCs has already occurred, much of their success remains a prediction as of this writing.

Despite the fact that they have been pronounced dead by various critics and pundits for years now, MOOCs continue to grow in terms of the number of both courses and participants. According to the MOOC news website Class Central, in 2014 there were 400 universities offering 2,400 different courses to an estimated 16 million to 18 million students (Shah 2014). By the end of 2016, Dhawal Shah reported in EdSurge that while "the spotlight on these companies" had "since dimmed" in recent years, they still are growing, with more than 58 million students participating in 6,850 courses offered by more than 700 participating universities and institutions all over the world (Shah 2016). As Cathy Davidson (2017b, 122) noted, Coursera alone had 25 million students start at least one course in 2016: "That's four million more students total than are enrolled in all colleges and universities in the United States today." So, while MOOCs are not going to *replace* institutional education and universities, they will continue to have a significant influence, and they are likely to continue in one form or another outside of higher education.

*MOOCs Helped Change the Discussion about the Value of*
*Higher Education and the Use of Technology in Teaching*

MOOCs demonstrated that there is high demand for education and also for changing (albeit slightly) some faculty practices and long-held perceptions about pedagogy. Davidson wrote a 2013 HASTAC blog post titled "If MOOCs Are the Answer, What Is the Question?" to remind her readers that a year or two before MOOCs captured the attention of the mainstream media, those same media outlets and pundits were openly questioning whether it was "worth it" to attend college: "These articles (I bet there were dozens if not hundreds) were often filled with hard data about the soaring costs of higher education and horrific student debt pitted against anecdotes of unemployment among the college educated. It was virtually a meme, that if you are fool enough to go to college, you end up deeper in debt and unemployed and therefore college isn't worth it. The tone in the press emphasized that latter point, demeaning the importance of higher education, laughing slyly at anyone who thinks higher education is a worthy goal." The high demand for and interest in MOOCs, Davidson (2013) argued, changed the answer to the question "is higher education worth it" to "a resounding, powerful 'yes' . . . People WANT higher learning. Period." Indeed, I'd argue that while few people completed the courses, the fact that MOOCs attracted so many initial users is good evidence that there is a demand for higher education *despite* all the well-documented problems associated with it.

The experiment of MOOCs has also shifted (though not entirely changed) many of my colleagues' assumptions about the validity of online courses generally. As I have said often in this book, online courses can be just as effective as face-to-face classes, though with different affordances. Before MOOCs, the majority of my colleagues would have disagreed with me. After MOOCs? I don't think everyone's minds about the value of online courses have changed, and, as was clear in the interviews I conducted for chapter 4, even a lot of professors who developed and taught MOOCs still believe face-to-face classes are "better" than online classes. At the same time, there is a growing acknowledgment that online courses done well can be effective, and there has been a noticeable increase in faculty wanting to experiment with new approaches like hybrid and flipped classrooms. This was evident in the faculty interviews I conducted, and it is also something Karen Head (2017, 160–161) writes about in *Disrupt This*:

> MOOCs have inspired professors, myself included, to incorporate more technology into their teaching practices. For example, if bad weather causes a campus closure, my MOOC experience has helped me to be more comfortable recording a lesson and distributing it to my students. I am confident about arranging for classes to meet virtually—something that is fairly easy with fifteen to thirty students. MOOCs have taught me to use technology to free up class time for those things that I can do with students . . . which means I do not have [to] use class time to disseminate material. Instead, I can sit with students while they work on their project, giving them immediate feedback . . . Essentially, MOOCs helped me consider my teaching practices through a new lens, which allowed me to revise (or augment) my practices to strengthen my effectiveness as a teacher.

*MOOCs Have Sparked Discussion and Innovation in Their "Afterlives"*

The 2012–2013 version of MOOCs—both in their design and their perceived threat to higher education—is gone, but the original MOOCs have left behind a host of descendants and possibilities. Many of these are introduced and described in the collection edited by Elizabeth Losh, *MOOCs and Their Afterlives: Experiments in Scale and Access in Higher Education* (2017). I'd highly recommend this collection to anyone interested in a sampling of what MOOC-inspired distance education might look like in the present and the near future. There is the turn back to what goes by the acronym SPOC for small private online courses, which seem to me to be similar to the traditional online courses I discuss at the end of chapter 2 and that have been a part of my teaching for some time. There is the CLMOOC, or connected learning massive open online collaboration Mia Zamora describes in her essay as a discussion and professional development space for teachers involved in the National Writing Project. There are the ongoing experiments of a DOCC, or distributed online collaborative course, described in Adeline Koh's essay "Feminist Pedagogy in the Digital Age: Experimenting between MOOCs and DOCCs." DOCCs exist as less a top-down/lecture-driven learning experience and more a collective of smaller courses—both face-to-face and online—that offer the opportunity to share discussions about common readings and exercises in a collaborative space. And there is also what Jessie Daniels, Polly Thistlethwaite, and Shawn(ta) Smith-Cruz describe as a POOC, or Participatory Open Online Course, an online space designed more for local (a campus or neighborhood community, for example) rather than global participation (Losh 2017).

In addition to these possibilities, I return to the idea of a MOOC as a textbook. I discussed this in chapter 3, particularly in relation to my own experiences of incorporating the EDC MOOC into my graduate course on "Computers and Writing," and it is easy for me to imagine something similar for first-year writing. With hundreds of thousands of students enrolled in freshman comp courses every semester in the United States, there seems ample opportunity to create a space where students and instructors from hundreds of different universities might be able to connect, discuss common readings, seek help from one another, and engage in peer review activities. And as I also observed with my more recent experiences as a MOOC student, MOOC providers have shifted from emphasizing "courses" with a "massive" number of enrolled students to individual and on-demand experiences. Essentially, these are textbooks, albeit ones delivered electronically and with some instructor support—for a fee, of course.

*MOOC Providers Have Shifted Their Emphasis Away*
*from Higher Education (Success TBA)*

The major MOOC providers are still partnering with major universities to develop courses, and many of those courses are still similar in some ways to courses offered at those universities. But rather than pursuing the strategy to attract traditional undergraduates, the providers have shifted direction and now offer courses and groups of courses with a variety of different names (for example, Udacity's "Nanodegree," Coursera's "Specializations," and edX's "MicroMasters") for a fee. MOOC providers have also partnered with corporations to offer training for existing employees and also created partnerships "in collaboration with" and as "hiring partners": for example, Udacity's Digital Marketing Nanodegree is offered in "collaboration with" Facebook, Google, Hootsuite, and others. For $999 (in 2018), enrollees in the "Career Advancement" Nanodegree Program receive what Udacity describes as a "full-immersion, full-feature learning experience." For $599, enrollees in the "Independent Study" self-study program pursue a "lean, curriculum-only opportunity."

In addition to no longer being "open" and "free," the courses are increasingly not "massive," since they are being offered as individualized, on-demand courses. These MOOCs (if that's still the right name for them) are designed for and marketed to professionals who either already have a bachelor's degree or who don't need a traditional college credential—which is to say, the big MOOC providers have shifted their emphasis away from higher education to professional development, and they are trying to make their courses more specifically useful for the audience of degree-holding professionals who originally enrolled in MOOCs in the first place.

Whether these fee-based programs will sustain companies like Coursera and Udacity remains to be seen. On the one hand, Shah (2016) said in his review of MOOC statistics and trends that the "big three" MOOC providers "combined have potentially made around $100 million in 2016," and Udacity has been profitable since 2015. A report by Assaf Gilad (2017) from the market research firm Zirra suggested that MOOC providers have yet to find a sustainable business model, though there is some promise: "In 2015, it was estimated that roughly 8% of companies use MOOCs for corporate training, while another 7% consider experimenting with MOOCs," and Coursera is expecting the demand for its services to triple in the next two years. If that interest in using MOOCs for professional development manifests itself and continues, perhaps many more college graduates will take their first MOOC when they start their careers.

## TWO PREDICTIONS AND A WARNING ABOUT
## THE FUZZY FUTURE AFTER MOOCS

One of the most important things I've learned from my accidental journey into scholarship about MOOCs over the past few years is that most predictions about the future of education and MOOCs have been wrong. So, in these closing pages, it would be foolish (or incredibly brave) of me to step too far out on a limb in predicting the next "big thing." The truth is, no one knows. However, I am confident in making two predictions and sounding one warning about what is liable to happen in the foreseeable future.

### Prediction 1: Higher Education Is Not Going to Be "Disrupted"
### or Become "the University of Everywhere"

Predictions of the "dramatic disruption" and fall of institutional education and universities come with the same regularity and poetic zeal of would-be prophets predicting the end of the world. Udacity's place as one of the ten remaining universities in the world and Clayton Christensen's predictions of mass university bankruptcies are just two examples that have gotten much attention in the mainstream media. Myths like this are enticing and make for good copy. As Audrey Watters (2013) has pointed out, such predictions are myths in two different yet curiously related senses of the word. These predictions are demonstrably false; but at the same time, Christensen and his ilk are creating a mythos that, like religion or faith, becomes "widely accepted as *unassailably* true" (Watters 2013, original emphasis).

Such myth making opens up the possibilities for the likes of Kevin Carey's (2016, 5) fantasy prediction of the future "University of Everywhere." Among many other platitudes, he argues:

> The University of Everywhere is where students of the future will go to college . . . Educational resources that have been scarce and expensive for centuries will be abundant and free . . . The University of Everywhere will span the earth. The students will come from towns, cities, and countries in all cultures and societies, members of a growing global middle class who will transform the experience of higher education . . . The University of Everywhere will solve the basic problem that has bedeviled universities since they were first invented over a millennium ago: how to provide a personalized, individual education to large numbers of people at a reasonable price.

I am confident that none of this is going to happen in my lifetime, in the lifetime of any of my current students, or in the lifetime of any of my current students' children. A century or so from now, the *Times Higher Education* list of the top 100 universities in the world will look very similar to the way the list looks now, and the rules David Labaree describes for the hierarchy of higher education will still be in place.

Things will be different, of course, and higher education will continue to change—albeit often at a pace more akin to "evolution" than "disruption." We will see more online courses and degree programs that break down the barriers among different universities—the "unbundling" of higher education. The funding of public higher education will continue to be volatile. More colleges and universities will close or merge, and those closures and mergers are more likely to impact less monied and less prestigious institutions like Eastern Michigan. We will continue to change the ways we offer courses, what subjects students study or don't study, and so forth. In much the same way many of us might be puzzled by some of the details of how higher education worked in the nineteenth century in America—with its mix of high schools, seminaries, colleges, and universities—I am sure that twenty-second-century scholars of higher education will be puzzled by the details of how higher education worked in the early twenty-first century. However, I am confident that the institutions of higher education will both continue to change and continue to be recognizable as universities. Institutional education is not going to cease to exist, and no one will be attending the amorphous "University of Everywhere."

*Prediction 2: The Shape of the Hierarchy Pyramid of Higher Education in the United States Might Change for the Worse*

Obviously, I find Labaree's articulation of the hierarchical stratification of higher education in the United States to be a compelling and correct description of the system, though it certainly isn't a fair and equitable system. The rich are still getting richer:

> Since schooling has come to be the primary way we decide who gets which job, this means gaining greater access to schooling at ever higher levels of the educational system. At the same time, however, in a liberal economy, where a high degree of social inequality is the norm, people who enjoy social advantages are eager to preserve these advantages and pass them on to their children. And, since we tend to award the best jobs to those with the best education, this means providing these children with privileged access to the most rewarding levels of schooling.
>
> What happens if you put the two elements together? You find that, when access to schooling increases, so does the stratification of schooling. More students come in at the bottom of the system in order to gain

social access, and the system keeps expanding upward in order to preserve social advantage. Levels of education rise but social differences remain the same. (Labaree 2017, 96)

In other words, the paradox of the increasing importance of and expanding access to higher education is that it allows those at the bottom to advance in terms of social class and economic status, and it simultaneously assures that those at the top will stay there.

What I worry about are the ways online courses and programs (MOOCs or their progeny) might further expand the distance between the bottom and the top of the pyramid. As it is currently, institutions at the bottom are more likely to have students in online courses and degree programs, and, in the interest of attracting students and maintaining enrollments, third-tier/regional universities tend to be much more accepting of transfer credits from other institutions than are the more selective and in-demand institutions at the top of the pyramid. MOOCs failed in part because students and their parents opted for established universities and decided that even free MOOCs weren't worth it. But if tuition continues to increase such that even the lowest-priced universities are out of the reach of working-class Americans, both students and institutions might have little choice but to reconsider something like MOOCs.

Greg Graham (2012) noted this fear early in the MOOC moment. Much as I am doing here, Graham asks his readers to cast their minds twenty or thirty or forty years into the future. With that in mind, it might not be difficult "to imagine a day when a face-to-face education could be a privilege of the elite." He goes on: "This could happen because the move toward online education is driven by a holy trinity of interests: state and local governments that want to reduce education expenditures, school administrators forced to cut budgets, and technology companies looking to expand their markets" (Graham 2012).

What could make this scenario even worse is if places like the University of Michigan continue to shy away from online courses and programs for their students while places like Eastern Michigan have little choice but to offer even more online courses and programs. Much in the way we live in an era where financial policies and tax reforms in the United States are resulting in wealth being concentrated among those in the top 1 percent or even the top 0.1 percent, we could have a future where the hierarchy pyramid in higher education in the United States grows both wider and taller. The result would be that the perceived value of a degree from a lower-tier university would decrease further while simultaneously increasing the perceived value of a degree from an elite university.

*And One Warning: The Lines between Nonprofit Institutions*
*of Higher Learning and For-Profit Educational Enterprises*
*Like Online Program Managers Will Blur Even More*

As both Abraham Flexner (1930) and David Noble (2001) made clear in their critiques, there has always been a problematic relationship between nonprofit universities and for-profit businesses. This has always been especially true with distance education, beginning with correspondence study. The proponents of distance education have been simultaneously motivated by a sincere desire to extend access to higher education *and* by the motive to make money, and the MOOC moment may have represented a new high (or a new low) for these conflicting motivations. The arrangements—financial and otherwise—between the for-profit MOOC providers and their nonprofit university partners are no longer on the front page of the higher education trade publications. But these problematic relationships persist, and they are likely to continue in much more far-reaching and thus potentially more problematic ways with the increased presence of Online Program Management firms.

Online Program Management companies (OPMs) pre-date MOOCs and, broadly speaking, they include companies like Blackboard Inc. and Instructure, both of which provide universities with Learning Management Systems—Blackboard and Canvas, for example. But in more recent years, OPMs have been expanding their businesses beyond providing straightforward technologies and services. As Phil Hill (2016) described it on his education consulting company's blog *e-Literate,* OPMs now "help nonprofit schools develop online programs, most often for master's level programs . . . Some examples of the services include marketing and recruitment, enrollment management, curriculum development, online course design, student retention support, technology hosting, and student and faculty support." Already a $1.5 billion business, Margaret Mattes (2017) reported that the estimated growth rate of the sector is "35 percent in the coming years." Mattes notes that 70 percent of the institutions that responded to her request for information reported that they had at least some relationship with an OPM "to facilitate their online programming," and her report goes on to describe dozens of these relationships between little-known OPMs and well-known universities all over the United States (Mattes 2017).

The OPM sector is changing in part because of changes underway in the proprietary school sector and online programs. While the for-profit University of Phoenix continues to lose students (Lindsay McKenzie reported that enrollments in 2018 had dropped below 100,000 students, though the University of Phoenix declined to comment on the accuracy of this claim), nonprofit online institutions are growing. Western Governors University, Southern New Hampshire University, and Liberty University—each a nonprofit but private university—have online programs with between 85,000 and 100,000 students. Higher education analyst Trace Urdan said that "government scrutiny, negative media coverage and self-inflicted scandals have created the impression that for-profits can't be trusted," and institutions like Southern New Hampshire that emphasize its nonprofit status in marketing are benefiting. Some other larger and public universities not known for their online offerings seem to be positioning themselves to take advantage of the falling reputations of proprietary schools as well (cited in McKenzie 2018).

In an evolving and controversial move, Purdue University acquired Kaplan University, further blurring the line between nonprofit (and state-supported) universities and for-profit providers and OPMs. According to Paul Fain (2017), "The new online university is slated to become a separately accredited nonprofit within the public Purdue system," which essentially means that the former Kaplan will provide many of the services of an OPM to Purdue. Publicly traded for-profit Grand Canyon University, which enrolls about 70,000 students online, is seeking permission from various regulators to convert to a nonprofit institution. "Industry analysts and lawyers said as many as 12 proposed for-profit conversions or sales are in the works," deals that are not necessarily as large as Purdue's acquisition but ones that could involve more public and nonprofit universities (Fain 2017).

A lot of the growth in the OPM sector is likely to come from institutions in the upper Midwest and the Northeast, where demographic predictions and their impact on enrollment are grim. A 2018 internal document circulated by EMU's administration notes that the number of high school graduates in the state of Michigan has declined 15.3 percent in the past ten years and is predicted to drop another 16 percent over the next ten years. At smaller liberal arts colleges and regional public universities like EMU, these demographic declines will mean drops in enrollment and thus in operating revenue.

Both Michigan State University and EMU were featured in the Mattes report as examples of institutions where OPM partnerships have been controversial and potentially deceiving. According to Mattes, MSU's online graduate programs offered through its Broad College of Business have "no indication that an external contractor (Bisk Education) provides recruitment and marketing services, as well as course production and instructional design for many of the programs rather than the university itself or that, for each dollar these programs bring in as revenue,

more than half goes to that contractor" (Mattes 2017). I'm more familiar with the controversy Mattes discusses at EMU with the agreement
between the university and Academic Partnerships (AP) to develop and
market a number of online programs, notably an "RN to BSN" degree.
These programs were in great demand in 2018, since regulatory and
other changes in the United States mean that most registered nurses
who have been practicing for years will soon need a Bachelor of Science
in Nursing. The agreement between the administration and AP—made
without faculty input—led to a dispute between the administration and
the faculty union that was ultimately resolved in a labor arbitration.
Essentially, the union argued that the agreement violated contractual
language about faculty governance and input, while the administration's
defense was that the agreement with AP was only about marketing and
thus was not a violation of the contract. But the larger issue for faculty
was concern about what the union fears is the "outsourcing" of instruction, curriculum, and other aspects of EMU's core mission.

The faculty were also concerned specifically about AP and its founder,
Randy Best. Unlike the founders behind the for-profit MOOC providers,
Best is not an educator who moved into business. Rather, he is an entre-
preneur who has been involved in many different businesses (including
a company that manufactured Girl Scout cookies) who became involved
in the education sector, first with K–12 schooling and then universities.
Patrick Michels (2016) chronicles Best's rise with a tutoring company
called Voyager that won large contracts to enact "No Child Left Behind"
initiatives based on "Best's well-placed friends, not on academic mer-
its." Michels (2016) said Best's critics later "called his company the
Halliburton of K–12 education. Now, they worry that for all of Best's
well-intentioned rhetoric, he's building the Blackwater of higher ed."

For this chapter I spoke briefly with administrators at both MSU and
EMU about their OPM agreements. Coincidentally, one of the MOOC
faculty I interviewed for chapter 4, Jeff Grabill, is currently MSU's associate provost for teaching, learning, and technology; and we met to talk
about MSU's relationship with Bisk. I also spoke to Kevin Kucera, vice
president and chief enrollment officer, about EMU's arrangement with
AP. Both were adamant that the deals with for-profit OPMs were not
interfering with the nonprofit institutional missions. Kucera emphasized again and again that EMU's relationship with AP was limited to
marketing, insisting that the students recruited by AP were "EMU students taking EMU classes taught by EMU faculty." Grabill also took issue
with the implication in Mattes's article that the MSU business faculty
members weren't involved in the teaching of the courses. While Bisk

lent its expertise to developing and designing the courses, Grabill said the implication in Mattes's article that the OPM was also teaching the courses "is just factually wrong."

One of the main critiques of these arrangements is the high cost of this marketing. Typically, and with both of these examples, OPMs collect about half of the tuition for students enrolled in online programs being marketed, which, over the time of the contracts, amounts to millions of dollars. For most faculty (myself included), giving away half of a course's tuition revenue doesn't make sense. But both Kucera and Grabill defended the costs, essentially because good marketing is expensive. "Faculty understand that (the agreements with OPMs) are giving away half the tuition, (but) they have no understanding of what they're buying and the value of that. If you execute, if you deliver on what the outcomes are supposed to be, then it's worth it," Grabill said, noting that universities typically do not have the marketing expertise of OPMs or the resources these companies are willing to invest at the beginning of the contracts with universities in terms of developing course materials and curriculum. All of the faculty I interviewed who developed and taught MOOCs noted the costs associated with producing their courses, and I presume those costs are similar for these online courses and programs. In that sense, Grabill argued, the arrangement universities make with OPMs is not unlike the arrangement most Americans use to buy a house: the amount of money borrowers pay in interest over the lifetime of a mortgage is much more than the initial purchase price of the house, but for most of us, that's the price of home ownership.

Ultimately, the arbitration at EMU was decided in favor of the administration in that the arbitrator agreed that the agreement with AP was about marketing and not curriculum, though the arbitrator also noted that future decisions should include the faculty in the process. So far, the main EMU program that has been marketed through AP has been the RN to BSN Online degree. There are plans for other online programs as well, including a Bachelor's in General Studies, designed in part to appeal to the large population of Americans with some college credits but no degree.

Both Grabill and Kucera said their institution's marketing efforts with OPMs have been successful so far. While we didn't discuss enrollment specifics, Grabill said the growth of the online programs offered through MSU's Broad College of Business and Bisk has been steady, and the students in the online programs represent a different demographic than those in more traditional and face-to-face programs. Kucera said there's been a rise in enrollment in EMU's RN to BSN Online program as AP has become more involved, though he was less specific about the Bachelor's in General Studies program. That said, Kucera also noted that the enrollment potential of the RN to BSN Only program will only last five or six more years as the number of nurses interested in converting their RN degrees to a BSN declines. So, while these partnerships with OPMs have helped increase enrollment at both institutions, the modest number of students in the programs is not enough to counter the decline in the number of on-campus students.

I appreciate both Grabill's and Kucera's insistence that these agreements with for-profit OPMs are only about marketing and do not endanger the mission or credibility of the institutions. But for would-be students, the line between the universities offering the program of study and the OPMs hired by universities is not clear. As Mattes noted, MSU's online graduate programs in business do not appear to be directly hosted on MSU's servers—the web address is michiganstateonline.com, and I presume it is managed directly by Bisk (Mattes).

The line between EMU and the OPM the institution has under contract is also fuzzy. The website for EMU's RN to BSN Online program appears to be hosted on EMU's campus servers, and it prominently features a space where would-be students can supply contact information or call a toll-free number for more information. Curious, I called the number in May 2018. After an automated message thanked me for contacting "Eastern Michigan University," my call was routed to a customer service representative who identified herself as working for EMU. I told the representative I was researching OPMs and asked if she actually worked for Eastern or for Academic Partnerships. Perhaps because she was afraid of being overheard going off-script, she replied "um, the second one." To summarize: a customer service representative in a call center (which could have been located anywhere on the planet) who was employed by a company based in Texas identified herself as a representative of a university located in southeast Michigan, and the only reason she noted that she actually worked for AP was because I asked her directly. I find that disconcerting.

I don't want to suggest that partnerships between nonprofit universities and for-profit educational enterprises like Online Program Management firms are always wrong. OPMs have been around for a long time, and there are good reasons for universities to pursue these partnerships. At the same time, as Mattes (2017) notes in her analysis of the growing role of OPMs: "If institutions—public and nonprofit alike—are not careful to monitor these contractors, students and taxpayers who thought they were working with a relatively safe public institution may find that they have been taken advantage of by a for-profit company. More so than other contracting arrangements, OPMs represent the outsourcing of the core educational mission of public institutions of higher education, threatening the consumer-minded focus that results from the public control of schools."

MOOCs quickly threatened to upend universities as we know them and almost as quickly shifted away from institutional education to job training and other non-institutional learning experiences. Like correspondence courses, television courses, and the first wave of online courses, MOOCs began with grand promises and ultimately faded into something more modest.

But just as I was concluding the revision of this chapter, the *Chronicle of Higher Education* reported in May 2018 about a new initiative at WGU with the provocative headline "Here's How Western Governors U. Aims to Enroll a Million Students." According to the story by Goldie Blumenstyk (2018), WGU "has just created a stand-alone organization, WGU Advancement. It will raise money to create new degree programs, as well as new educational models designed to reach tens of millions of adults who need additional skills to succeed in the workforce." Like MOOCs, the promise is to offer credentials and training outside the structure of institutional education for the "large numbers of people who need different solutions." Like MOOCs, WGU Advancement is hoping to reach a massive number of students. Like MOOCs, WGU Advancement is simultaneously trying to help improve the lives of many would-be students *and* trying to profit from them. Like MOOCs, WGU Advancement is again hoping to disrupt higher education through a complicated mix of nonprofit and for-profit partnerships. Like MOOCs, the goal of enrolling a million students at one institution is to "change everything."

And the moment continues.

# REFERENCES

Agarwal, Anant. 2013. "Why Massively Open Online Courses (Still) Matter." *TED*. https://www.ted.com/talks/anant_agarwal_why_massively_open_online_courses_still_matter.

Allen, I. Elaine, and Jeff Seaman. 2015. *Grade Level: Tracking Online Education in the United States*. Babson Survey Research Group and Quahog Research Group, LLC. http://www.onlinelearningsurvey.com/reports/gradelevel.pdf.

Arenson, Karen. 1998. "More Colleges Plunging into Uncharted Waters of Online Courses." *New York Times*. November 2. http://www.nytimes.com/library/tech/98/11/biztech/articles/02online-education.html.

"Arizona State University Expands the Use of McGraw-Hill Education's ALEKS Artificial Intelligence Software in Its Global Freshman Academy." 2017. McGraw-Hill press release. May 30. https://www.mheducation.com/news-media/press-releases/asu-aleks-artificial-intelligence-global-freshman-academy.html.

Atkinson, Carroll. 1941. *Radio Extension Courses Broadcast for Credit*. Boston: Meador.

Bennett, Rebecca, and Mike Kent. 2017. "Any Colour as Long as It's Black! MOOCs, (Post)-Fordism, and Inequality" In *Massive Open Online Courses and Higher Education: What Went Right, What Went Wrong, and Where to Next*, ed. Rebecca Bennett and Mike Kent, 11–25. New York: Routledge.

Bidwell, Allie. 2015. "High School Graduation Rate Hits All-Time High." *US News and World Report*. February 12. http://www.usnews.com/news/blogs/data-mine/2015/02/12/us-high-school-graduation-rate-hits-all-time-high.

Bill and Melinda Gates Foundation. 2012. "Gates Foundation Awards $3 Million in Mooc Grants." *Communications of the ACM*. November 14. https://cacm.acm.org/careers/157392-gates-foundation-awards-3-million-in-mooc-grants/fulltext.

Bittner, Walton Simon, and Mervey Foster Mallory. 1933. *University Teaching by Mail: A Survey of Correspondence Instruction Conducted by American Universities*. New York: Macmillan.

Blumenstyk, Goldie. 2018. "Here's How Western Governors U. Aims to Enroll a Million Students." *Chronicle of Higher Education*. May 23. https://www.chronicle.com/article/Here-s-How-Western-Governors/243492.

Bogost, Ian. 2017. "The Secret Lives of MOOCs." In *MOOCs and Their Afterlives: Experiments in Scale and Access in Higher Education*, ed. Elizabeth Losh, 271–286. Chicago: University of Chicago Press.

Bonk, Curtis J., Mimi M. Lee, Thomas C. Reeves, and Thomas H. Reynolds, eds. 2015. *MOOCs and Open Education around the World*. New York. Routledge.

Carey, Kevin. 2016. *The End of College: Creating the Future of Learning and the University of Everywhere*. New York: Riverhead Books.

Chafkin, Max. 2013. "Udacity's Sebastian Thrun, Godfather of Free Online Education, Changes Course." *Fast Company*. November 14. http://www.fastcompany.com/3021473/udacity-sebastian-thrun-uphill-climb.

Chang, Heewon. 2008. *Autoethnogrpahy as Method*. Walnut Creek, CA: Left Coast Press.

Chapman, Gary. 1998. "Will Technology Commercialize Higher Learning?" *Los Angeles Times*. January 19. http://articles.latimes.com/1998/jan/19/business/fi-9788.

Comer, Denise. 2014. "Learning How to Teach . . . Differently: Extracts from a MOOC Instructor's Journal." In *Invasion of the MOOCs: The Promise and Perils of Massive Open*

*Online Courses*, ed. Steven D. Krause and Charles Lowe, 130–149. Anderson, SC: Parlor Press.

Comer, Denise, Ryan Baker, and Yuan Wang. 2015. "Negativity in Massive Online Open Courses: Impacts on Learning and Teaching and How Instructional Teams May Be Able to Address It." *InSight: A Journal of Scholarly Teaching* 10: 92–113. https://files.eric .ed.gov/fulltext/EJ1074060.pdf.

Comer, Denise, and Edward White. 2016. "Adventuring into MOOC Writing Assessment: Challenges, Results, and Possibilities." *College Composition and Communication* 67, no. 3: 318–359.

Davidson, Cathy N. 2013. "If MOOCs Are the Answer, What Is the Question?" HASTAC blog post. February 7. https://www.hastac.org/blogs/cathy-davidson/2013/02/07/if -moocs-are-answer-what-question.

Davidson, Cathy N. 2017a. "Connecting Learning: What I Learned from Teaching a Meta-MOOC." In *MOOCs and Their Afterlives: Experiments in Scale and Access in Higher Education*, ed. Elizabeth Losh, 67–75. Chicago: University of Chicago Press.

Davidson, Cathy N. 2017b. *The New Education: How to Revolutionize the University to Prepare Students for a World in Flux.* New York: Basic Books.

D'Onfro, Jillian. 2015. "The Founder of Google's Top Secret Project Lab Has a New Plan to Double the World's GDP." *Business Insider.* August 12. http://www.businessinsider .com/udacity-google-x-founder-sebastian-thrun-interview-2015-8.

Eagan, Kevin, Ellen Bara Stolzenberg, Hilary B. Zimmerman, Melissa C. Aragon, Hannah Whang Sauson, and Cecilia Rios-Aguilar. 2017. *The American Freshman: National Norms Fall 2016.* Los Angeles: Higher Education Research Institute. https://www.heri.ucla .edu/monographs/TheAmericanFreshman2016.pdf.

"Enrollment in Distance Education Courses, by State: Fall 2012." 2014. US Department of Education, National Center for Education Statistics. NCES 2014–023. http://nces.ed .gov/pubs2014/2014023.pdf.

Fain, Paul. 2017. "Federal Audit Challenges Faculty Role at WGU." *Inside Higher Ed.* September 22. https://www.insidehighered.com/news/2017/09/22/education-depts -inspector-general-calls-western-governors-repay-713-million-federal.

Flexner, Abraham. 1930. *Universities: American, English, German.* New York: Oxford University Press.

Gilad, Assaf. 2017. "A Deep Dive Analysis of Coursera." Zirra Market Analysis and Insights. May 4. https://wisdom.zirra.com/2017/05/04/a-deep-dive-analysis-of-coursera/.

Grabill, Jeffrey T. 2014. "Why We Are Thinking about MOOCs." In *Invasion of the MOOCs: The Promise and Perils of Massive Open Online Courses*, ed. Steven D. Krause and Charles Lowe, 39–44. Anderson, SC: Parlor Press.

Graham, Greg. 2012. "After the Buzz: How the Embrace of MOOCs Could Hurt Middle America." *Chronicle of Higher Education.* October 1. https://www.chronicle.com/article /After-the-Buzz-How-the/134654.

Harasim, Linda. 2000. "Shift Happens: Online Education as a New Paradigm in Learning." *Internet and Higher Education* 3: 41–61.

Harris, Sean Michael, and Jesse Stommel. 2017. "Open Education as Resistance: MOOCs and Critical Digital Pedagogy." In *MOOCs and Their Afterlives: Experiments in Scale and Access in Higher Education*, ed. Elizabeth Losh, 177–197. Chicago: University of Chicago Press.

Head, Karen. 2013. "Massive Open Online Adventure." *Chronicle of Higher Education.* April 23. https://www.chronicle.com/article/Massive-Open-Online-Adventure/138803.

Head, Karen. 2017. *Disrupt This! MOOCs and the Promises of Technology.* Lebanon, NH: University Press of New England.

Hess, Abigail. 2017. "Harvard Business School Professor: Half of American Colleges Will Be Bankrupt in 10 to 15 Years." *CNBC Website.* November 15. https://www.cnbc.com /2017/11/15/hbs-professor-half-of-us-colleges-will-be-bankrupt-in-10-to-15-years.html.

Hill, Phil. 2016. "Online Program Management: A View of the Market Landscape." *e-Literate blog*. June 8. https://mfeldstein.com/online-enablers-a-landscape-view-of-the-market-for-higher-education/.

"The Hype Is Dead, but MOOCs Are Marching On." 2015. *Knowledge@Wharton*. January 5. http://knowledge.wharton.upenn.edu/article/moocs-making-progress-hype-died/.

James, Melanie. 2017. "Autoethnography: The Story of 'Doing a MOOC' or Knowing 'the Beast' from Within." In *Massive Open Online Courses and Higher Education: What Went Right, What Went Wrong, and Where to Next*, ed. Rebecca Bennett and Mike Kent, 77–91. New York: Routledge.

Jaschik, Scott. 2015. "Not a Tsunami, But . . ." *Inside Higher Ed*. March 16. https://www.insidehighered.com/news/2015/03/16/stanford-president-offers-predictions-more-digital-future-higher-education.

Kearney, Melissa S., and Phillip B. Levine. 2015a. "Early Childhood Education by MOOC: Lessons from *Sesame Street*." NBER Working Paper 21229. http://www.nber.org/papers/w21229.

Kearney, Melissa S., and Phillip B. Levine. 2015b. "What the Media Got Wrong about Our 'Sesame Street' Education Study." *New Republic*. June 19. https://newrepublic.com/article/122084/what-media-got-wrong-about-our-sesame-street-education-study.

Kett, Joseph F. 1994. *The Pursuit of Knowledge under Difficulties: From Self-Improvement to Adult Education in America, 1750–1990*. Stanford, CA: Stanford University Press.

Khosla, Varuni. 2017. "Udacity to Focus on Individual Student Projects." *Economic Times*. October 6. https://economictimes.indiatimes.com/industry/services/education/udacity-to-focus-on-individual-student-projects/articleshow/60963078.cms.

Kim, Joshua. 2012. "4 Reasons Why the Bonk MOOC Is So Interesting." *Inside Higher Ed*. April 25. https://www.insidehighered.com/blogs/technology-and-learning/4-reasons-why-bonk-mooc-so-interesting.

Knox, Jeremy, Sian Bayne, Hamish MacLeod, Jen Ross, and Christine Sinclair. 2012. "MOOC Pedagogy: The Challenges of Developing for Coursera." *#ALTC Blog*. Association for Learning Technology. August 8. https://altc.alt.ac.uk/blog/2012/08/mooc-pedagogy-the-challenges of developing-for-coursera/#gref.

Koller, Daphne. 2012. "What We're Learning from Online Education." *TED*. https://www.ted.com/talks/daphne_koller_what_we_re_learning_from_online_education.

Kolowich, Steve. 2013. "A University's Offer of Credit for a MOOC Gets No Takers." *Chronicle of Higher Education*. July 8. https://www.chronicle.com/article/A-Universitys-Offer-of-Credit/140131.

Krause, Steven D. *stevendkrause.com*. http://stevendkrause.com.

Krause, Steven D. 2013. "MOOC Response about 'Listening to World Music.'" *College Composition and Communication* 64, no. 4: 689–695.

Krause, Steven D. 2014. "MOOC Assigned." In *Invasion of the MOOCs: The Promise and Perils of Massive Open Online Courses*, ed. Steven D. Krause and Charles Lowe, 122–129. Anderson, SC: Parlor Press.

Krause, Steven D. 2017. "Always Alone and Together: Three of My MOOC Student Discussion and Participation Experiences." In *MOOCs and Their Afterlives: Experiments in Scale and Access in Higher Education*, ed. Elizabeth Losh, 241–252. Chicago: University of Chicago Press.

Krause, Steven D., and Charles Lowe, eds. 2014. *Invasion of the MOOCs: The Promises and Perils of Massive Open Online Courses*. Anderson, SC: Parlor Press.

Labaree, David F. 2017. *A Perfect Mess: The Unlikely Ascendancy of American Higher Education*. Chicago: University of Chicago Press.

Leckart, Steven. 2012. "The Stanford Education Experiment Could Change Higher Learning Forever." *WIRED*. March 20. http://www.wired.com/wired-science/2012/03/ff_aiclass/all/.

Lewin, Tamar. 2012. "A Class Where Opening Minds, Not Earning Credits, Is the Point." *New York Times.* November 19. http://www.nytimes.com/2012/11/20/education/on line-course-opens-minds-to-world-music.html?_r=0.

Losh, Elizabeth, ed. 2017. *MOOCs and Their Afterlives: Experiments in Scale and Access in Higher Education.* Chicago: University of Chicago Press.

"Manifesto for Teaching Online." 2011. http://www.swop.education.ed.ac.uk/edinburgh _manifesto_onlineteaching.pdf.

"Massive Open Online Courses (MOOCs)." Press release. 2012. Bill and Melinda Gates Foundation. November 13. http://www.gatesfoundation.org/postsecondaryeducation /Pages/massive-open-online-courses.aspx.

Mattes, Margaret. 2017. "The Private Side of Public Higher Education." *Century Foundation.* August 7. https://tcf.org/content/report/private-side-public-higher-education/.

Matulis, Anthony Stanley. 1938. "A Study of the Supervised College Correspondence Study Department as Sponsored by the Extension Division of the University of Michigan." MA thesis, University of Michigan, Ann Arbor.

"McGraw-Hill Education's ALEKS Adaptive Software Will Be Used in ASU's Global Freshman Academy." 2016. *McGraw-Hill Education.* April 18. https://www.mheducation .com/news-media/press-releases/asu-global-freshman-academy-aleks-mcgraw-hill -education.html.

McKenzie, Lindsay. 2018. "The 100K Club." *Inside Higher Ed.* April 23. https://www .insidehighered.com/news/2018/04/23/nonprofits-poised-unseat-u-phoenix-largest -online-university.

Michels, Patrick. 2016. "Randy Best Is Going to Save Texas' Public Universities, or Get Rich Trying." *Texas Observer.* August 29. https://www.texasobserver.org/randy-best-is-going -to-save-texas-public-universities-or-get-rich-trying/.

Milligan, Sandra K. 2013. "Better than a Tarantino Movie: Raw Peer Assessment in #edcmooc." *Sandra's Exploration of On-Line Learning.* May 3. https://sandrakmilligan .wordpress.com/2013/03/05/better-than-a-tarantino-movie-raw-peer-assessment-in-a -mooc/.

Moe, Rolin. 2015. "What the Researchers Got Wrong about Their 'Sesame Street' Education Study." *All MOOCs, All the Time.* June 22. https://allmoocs.wordpress.com/2015 /06/22/what-the-researchers-got-wrong-about-their-sesame-street-education-study/.

Moore, Michael, and Greg Kearsley. 2005. *Distance Education: A Systems View.* Second ed. Belmont, CA: Thomson Wadsworth.

Murphy, Judith, and Ronald Gross. 1966. *Learning by Television.* New York: Fund for the Advancement of Education.

Myers, Courtney Boyd. 2011. "Clayton Christensen: Why Online Education Is Ready for Disruption, Now." *The Next Web.* November 13. https://thenextweb.com/insider/ 2011/11/13/clayton-christensen-why-online-education-is-ready-for-disruption-now/.

"New Precalculus Course Is the Second Math Course Offered after College Algebra and Problem Solving Launched a Year Ago." 2017. *McGraw-Hill Education.* May 30. https:// www.mheducation.com/news-media/press-releases/asu-aleks-artificial-intelligence -global-freshman-academy.html.

Noble, David F. 2001. *Digital Diploma Mills: The Automation of Higher Education.* New York: Monthly Review Press.

Noor, Mohamed. 2013. "Flipping with a MOOC—a Very New Approach to Teaching for Me." *Science, Food, Etc.* May 4. https://science-and-food.blogspot.com/2013/05/flipping -with-mooc-very-new-approach-to.html.

Norvig, Peter. 2012. "The 100,000 Student Classroom." *TED.* February 2012. https://www .ted.com/talks/peter_norvig_the_100_000_student_classroom.

Odum, Stephanie, and Leslie Lindsey. 2016. "Hacking the Lecture: Transgressive Praxis and Presence Using Online Video." In *Handbook of Research on Writing and Composing in the Age of MOOCs*, ed. Elizabeth A. Monskey and Kristine L. Blair, 331–347. Hershey, PA: IGI Global.

Oremus, Will. 2013. "University Suspends Online Classes after More than Half the Students Fail." *Slate*. July. http://www.slate.com/blogs/future_tense/2013/07/19/san _jose_state_suspends_udacity_online_classes_after_students_fail_final.html.

"Our History." N.d. *Chautauqua Institution*. https://chq.org/about-us/history.

Pappano, Laura. 2012. "The Year of the MOOC." *New York Times*. November 2. http:// www.nytimes.com/2012/11/04/education/edlife/massive-open-online-courses-are -multiplying-at-a-rapid-pace.html.

Parr, Chris. 2013. "MOOC Creators Criticize Courses' Lack of Creativity." *Times Higher Education*. October 17. https://www.timeshighereducation.com/news/mooc-creators -criticise-courses-lack-of-creativity/2008180.article.

Purdy, Leslie N. 1980. "The History of Television and Radio in Continuing Education." *New Directions for Continuing Education* 5: 15–29.

Rao, Leena. 2016. "Sebastian Thrun Steps Down as Udacity's CEO." *Fortune.com*. April 22. http://fortune.com/2016/04/22/sebastian-thrun-udacity/.

Reed, Matt. 2015. "What Problems Are ASU and edX Solving?" *Inside Higher Ed*. April 23. https://www.insidehighered.com/blogs/confessions-community-college-dean/what -problem-are-asu-and-edx-solving.

Reed-Danahay, Deborah E., ed. 1997. *Auto/Ethnography: Rewriting the Self and the Social*. New York: Berg.

Reid, Alex. 2017. "The Prospects and Regrets of an EdTech Gold Rush." In *MOOCs and Their Afterlives: Experiments in Scale and Access in Higher Education*, ed. Elizabeth Losh, 227–240. Chicago: University of Chicago Press.

Rice, Jeff. 2013. "What I Learned in MOOCs." *College Composition and Communication* 64, no. 4: 695–703.

Rivard, Ry. 2013. "Udacity Project on 'Pause.'" *Inside Higher Ed*. July 18. http://www.inside highered.com/news/2013/07/18/citing-disappointing-student-outcomes-san-jose -state-pauses-work-udacity.

Selfe, Cynthia L., and Gail E. Hawisher. 2004. *Literate Lives in the Information Age: Narratives of Literacy from the United States*. Mahwah, NJ: Lawrence Erlbaum Associates.

Severance, Charles. 2015. "Learning about MOOCs by Talking to Students." In *MOOCs and Open Education around the World*, ed. Curtis J. Bonk, Mimi M. Lee, Thomas C. Reeves, and Thomas H. Reynolds, 169–179. New York: Routledge.

Shah, Dhawal. 2014. "Online Courses Raise Their Game: A Review of MOOC Stats and Trends in 2014." *Class Central*. December 27. https://www.class-central.com/report/ moocs-stats-and-trends-2014/.

Shah, Dhawal. 2016. "Monetization over Massiveness: Breaking down MOOCs by the Numbers in 2016." *EdSurge*. December 29. https://www.edsurge.com/news/2016-12-29 -monetization-over-massiveness-breaking-down-moocs-by-the-numbers-in-2016.

Shapiro, Deborah. 2015. "Archivist's Angle: The Sunrise and Sunset of 'Sunrise Semester.'" *NYU Alumni Connect*. September 15. http://www.alumni.nyu.edu/s/1068/2col_scripts .aspx?sid=1068&gid=1&pgid=11132.

Shepard, Richard. 1962. "TV Student Wins an NYU Diploma: Housewife's Interest Revived by 'Sunrise Semester.'" *New York Times*. May 19, L 55.

Shirky, Clay. 2015. "The Digital Revolution in Higher Education Has Already Happened. No One Noticed." *medium.com*. November 6. https://medium.com/@cshirky/the-digital -revolution-in-higher-education-has-already-happened-no-one-noticed-78ec0fec16c 7#.d7jzutzvf.

Siemens, George. 2012a. "MOOCs Are Really a Platform." *elearnspace*. July 25. http://www .elearnspace.org/blog/2012/07/25/moocs-are-really-a-platform/.

Siemens, George. 2012b. "More on Massive Open Online Courses." *elearnspace*. July 31. http://www.elearnspace.org/blog/2012/07/31/more-on-massive-open-online-courses/.

Straumsheim, Carl. 2015. "Less Than 1%." *Inside Higher Ed.* December 21. https://www
.insidehighered.com/news/2015/12/21/323-learners-eligible-credit-moocs-arizona
-state-u.

Stripling, Jack. 2009. "So Many Students, So Little Time." *Inside Higher Ed.* March 24.
https://www.insidehighered.com/news/2009/03/24/heh.

"Student Profile." 2017. University of Michigan undergraduate admissions website.
https://admissions.umich.edu/apply/freshmen-applicants/student-profile.

Sweeney, Isaac. 2013a. "Alone with Thousands of Other People." *Chronicle of Higher Education.* April 3. http://chronicle.com/blogs/onhiring/alone-with-thousands-of-other
-people/37513.

Sweeney, Isaac. 2013b. "Why I'm A Bad Student." *Chronicle of Higher Education.* June 14.
http://chronicle.com/blogs/onhiring/why-im-a-bad-student/39439.

Vincent, John Heyl. 1886. *The Chautauqua Movement.* Boston: Chautauqua Press. https://
books.google.com/books?id=lqsMAAAAYAAJ&printsec=frontcover&source=gbs_ge
_summary_r&cad=0#v=onepage&q&f=false.

Warner, John 2013. "I'm Failing My MOOC." *Inside Higher Ed.* April 22. https://www
.insidehighered.com/blogs/just-visiting/im-failing-my-mooc.

Watkins, Barbara L. 1991. "A Quite Radical Idea: The Invention and Elaboration of Collegiate Correspondence Study." In *The Foundations of American Distance Education: A
Century of Collegiate Correspondence Study,* ed. Barbara L. Watkins and Stephen J. Wright,
1–35. Dubuque, IA: Kendall/Hunt.

Watkins, Barbara L., and Stephen J. Wright, eds. 1991. *The Foundations of American Distance
Education: A Century of Collegiate Correspondence Study.* Dubuque, IA: Kendall/Hunt.

Watters, Audrey. 2013. "The Myth and Millennialism of Disruptive Innovation." *Hack Education.* May 24. http://hackeducation.com/2013/05/24/disruptive-innovation.

Watters, Audrey. 2015. "No, Sesame Street Was Not the First MOOC." *Hack Education.*
June 21. http://hackeducation.com/2015/06/21/sesame-street-is-not-a-mooc-ffs.

Young, Jeffrey R. 2012. "Inside the Coursera Contract: How an Upstart Company Might
Profit from Free Courses." *Chronicle of Higher Education.* July 19. https://www.chronicle
.com/article/How-an-Upstart-Company-Might/133065.

Young, Jeffrey R. 2013. "Coursera Announces Details for Selling Certificates and Verify-
ing Identities." *Chronicle of Higher Education.* January 9. http://chronicle.com/blogs
/wiredcampus/?p=41519?cid=wc&utm_source=wc&utm_medium=en.

Young, Jeffrey R. 2017. "Udacity Official Declares MOOCs 'Dead' (Though the Company
Still Offers Them)." *EdSurge.* October 13. https://www.edsurge.com/news/2017-10-12
-udacity-official-declares-moocs-dead-though-the-company-still-offers-them.

# ABOUT THE AUTHOR

**Steven D. Krause** is a professor in the Department of English Language and Literature at Eastern Michigan University in Ypsilanti. Most of his scholarship and teaching explores the connections among writing, rhetoric, pedagogy, and technology. Along with Charles Lowe, he co-edited the essay collection *Invasion of the MOOCs: The Promise and Perils of Massive Open Online Courses.*

# INDEX

AA degrees, 49

*Abelard to Apple: The Fate of American Colleges and Universities* (DeMillo), 27

Academic Partnerships (AP), 127, 128, 129

access, to higher education, 9, 20–21, 123–24

accreditation, 13

"Adventuring into MOOC Writing Assessment: Challenges, Results, and Possibilities" (Comer and White), 74, 75

Agarwal, Anant, 34

ALEKS. *See* Assessment and Learning in Knowledge Spaces

"Always Alone and Together: Three of My MOOC Student Discussion and Participation Experiences" (Krause), 69, 72–73, 78

*American Freshman: National Norms Fall 2016, The* (Eagan et al.), 31

anxieties, teaching, 96–100

AP. *See* Academic Partnerships

appearance, for videos, 98–100

Arenson, Karen, 55

Arizona State University: "English Composition 1," 73; Global Freshman Academy, 29, 79, 80, 81–82

artificial intelligence, 18

Assessment and Learning in Knowledge Spaces (ALEKS), and ASU courses, 81–83

Athabasca University, 17

Atkinson, Carroll, *Radio Extension Courses Broadcast for Credit*, 47–48

autoethnography, 57–58

Baker, Ryan, 106

Bayne, Sian, 69, 71

Bennett, Rebecca, 26, 59

Best, Randy, 127

Bisk Education, 126, 127–28

Bittner, Walton Simon, *University Teaching by Mail*, 42, 46

Blackboard, Inc., 58, 125

Blakesley, David, 4

Blancato, Michael, 85; on discussion forums, 112–13

Bletchley Park Museum, 78

blogs, 72; "English Composition 1," 76–77; "Listening to World Music," 59–60, 64–65

Blumenstyk, Goldie, "Here's How Western Governors U. Aims to Enroll a Million Students," 130

Bogost, Ian, 21

Bonk, Curtis J., 90; "Empowering Learning Through Community," 58

Brazil, online programs, 89

Broad College of Business (MSU), 126, 128

bulletin boards, online, 65

Burnett, Rebecca, 87

business model, MOOC, 30–31

California, 21

call centers, and OPMs, 129

Cal Tech, 28

*Cambridge Handbook of Expertise and Expert Performance*, 75

Canada, 15; CCK08, 17–18

Canvas, 125

"Career Advancement" Nanodegree Program, 121

Carey, Kevin, 21, 25, 122

Carnegie Classification of Institutions of Higher Education, 12

Carnegie Commission on Higher Education, 12

Carnegie Foundation, 44

Carr, Cora Gay, 48

CBS television, 48

CCK08. *See* Connectivism and Connective Knowledge

certifications, certificates, 12–13, 22, 30

Chang, Heewon, 57

Chapman, Gary, 54

Chausow, Hymen, *Chicago's TV College*, 49

Chautauqua College of Liberal Arts, 39, 41

Chautauqua Institution and Movement, 35–36; correspondence courses, 38–39